PRAISE FOR JAMES ALTUCHER

"James Altucher is scary smart."

— STEPHEN DUBNER, AUTHOR OF *FREAKONOMICS*

"What I like about James is you can tell he came from a roller coaster. He chose his own path to success without knowing the outcome. And . . . one thing is for sure: if you don't make courageous choices for yourself, nobody else will."

— DICK COSTOLO, CEO OF TWITTER

PRAISE FOR THE POWER OF NO

"Every 'no' makes space for the perfect 'yes.' It's impossible to thrive in an overcommitted world. And yet it's so easy to get caught up—to drain our energy bank account, leaving us mentally, physically, and spiritually bankrupt. Your freedom may be closer than you think. The Power of No by James and Claudia Altucher is an invitation to a universe of meaningful opportunities on the other side of 'no.' I'm so grateful for this book and I know you will be too."

— KRIS CARR, *NEW YORK TIMES* BEST-SELLING AUTHOR OF *CRAZY SEXY KITCHEN*

"The Power of No *takes a fresh approach to becoming masterful at using 'no' to say 'yes' to life. Grounded in both practical and spiritual wisdom, James and Claudia take the reader on an unexpected journey that explores a variety of ways we prevent ourselves from being fully present in the here and now. Their book is filled with magic that can change your life if you're brave enough to follow their lead!*"

— CHERYL RICHARDSON, *NEW YORK TIMES* BEST-SELLING AUTHOR OF *THE ART OF EXTREME SELF-CARE*

"*I would recommend this book to any member of the human species. It's bold, empowering, and useful. It gave me the courage to turn down distractions so that I could focus on the important things in life, like endorsing this book.*"

— A. J. JACOBS, *NEW YORK TIMES* BEST-SELLING AUTHOR OF *DROP DEAD HEALTHY*

THE
POWER
OF
NO

ALSO BY JAMES ALTUCHER

Choose Yourself: Be Happy, Make Millions, Live the Dream

FAQ Me

How to Be the Luckiest Person Alive!

I Was Blind but Now I See

ALSO BY CLAUDIA AZULA ALTUCHER

21 Things to Know Before Starting an Ashtanga Yoga Practice

THE
POWER
OF
NO

BECAUSE ONE LITTLE WORD CAN BRING
HEALTH, ABUNDANCE, AND HAPPINESS

JAMES ALTUCHER
AND
CLAUDIA AZULA ALTUCHER

HAY
HOUSE

HAY HOUSE, INC.

Carlsbad, California • New York City
London • Sydney • New Delhi

Published in the United States by: Hay House, Inc.: www.hayhouse.com®
• *Published in Australia by:* Hay House Australia Pty. Ltd.: www.hayhouse.com. au • *Published in the United Kingdom by:* Hay House UK, Ltd.: www.hayhouse. co.uk • *Published in India by:* Hay House Publishers India: www.hayhouse.co.in

Cover design: Michelle Polizzi • *Interior design: Celia Fuller-Vels*

The authors of this book do not dispense medical advice or prescribe the use of any technique as a form of treatment for physical, emotional, or medical problems without the advice of a physician, either directly or indirectly. The intent of the authors is only to offer information of a general nature to help you in your quest for emotional and spiritual well-being. In the event you use any of the information in this book for yourself, the authors and the publisher assume no responsibility for your actions.

Library of Congress Cataloging-in-Publication Data

Altucher, James.
 The power of no : because one little word can bring health, abundance, and happiness / James Altucher and Claudia Azula Altucher. -- 1st edition.
   pages cm
   ISBN 978-1-4019-4587-9 (paperback)
 1. Self-esteem. 2. Conduct of life. 3. Self-realization. 4. Success. 5. Happiness. I. Altucher, Claudia Azula. II. Title.
 BJ1533.S3.A48 2014
 158.1--dc23

                                                                    2014011685

Tradepaper ISBN: 978-1-4019-4587-9
E-Book ISBN: 978-1-4019-4676-0
Audiobook ISBN: 978-1-4019-4738-5

14 13 12 11 10 9 8 7 6 5
1st edition, July 2014

Printed in the United States of America

To Eckhart Tolle
for inspiring us with the first twelve letters of his bestseller

and

to the reader
for not saying NO to reading this book

CONTENTS

YOUR NO
BILL OF RIGHTS

No is an incredibly painful, brave word to say.

How many times have you had to say no only to have it cause anguish, desperation, arguments, and anxiety?

Even the hours, days, and months before you say no are filled with anxiety: "Should I?" "Could I?" "What will happen?"

But you have the right to say no. In fact, you have a whole Bill of Rights. These rights are already yours. This book will help you fully realize them.

1 You Have the Right to Defend Your Life

You are entitled to say NO to the things that will directly hurt you: fire, jumping off a building, drinking poison, overdosing.

People readily say no to something as extreme and dramatic as fire. But other No's are more subtle. It might be harder to say no to cigarettes, alcohol, or toxic relationships. You decide what you say no to. Nobody else does.

2 You Have the Right to Healthy Relationships and Real Love

You decide *whom* you say NO to. You are entitled to choose your tribe, regardless of what society imposes on you. You decide who in your life drains you of energy, and then purge them so you can soar. This does not mean you become a hermit; it means you choose your family, your friends, your colleagues, your tribe, *your life*.

3 You Have the Right to Use Your Talents and Allow Abundance into Your Life

You are entitled to say NO to whatever gets in the way of your creative force and keeps it from bringing you a life of abundance. You are uniquely needed in this world, but only if you say no to the barricades.

You have a mission. Only you can give the gift you have. You deserve abundance, wealth, and appreciation for your work.

4 You Have the Right to Assert What You Want

Every day, colleagues, institutions, bosses, friends, and family want you to attend to their needs. They don't do this because they are bad or selfish. They do this because it is simply what people do; they have their own best interests at heart.

And you are also entitled to have your best interests at heart. You don't have to do what everyone else in society is doing. You are a unique combination of DNA, environment, culture, and personal experiences. For you to say yes to something, it has to be special to *you*.

Everything else, no matter what the consequences, you are entitled to say NO to.

When you say yes to something you don't want to do, here is the result: you hate what you are doing, you resent the person who asked you, and you hurt yourself.

5 You Have the Right to Choose What Stories You Believe In

Why did humans move up the food chain 70,000 years ago? Because we developed the language to tell stories. Stories, myths, religions, and institutions allow us to cooperate with millions of other humans.

Humans are great storytellers. That's what separates us from every other species. There are thousands of common stories that are baked into our societal mythology and that we believe are real. Some of them are: College. Owning a home. Marriage. Children. Having a cushy job. Postponing our dreams for when there will be money. "Work hard and succeed!" Ten thousand hours to mastery. And so on.

You are entitled to say NO to the stories that do not serve your own evolution, and yes only to the ones that align with your spiritual work, your bliss, and your ability to manifest a fulfilling life.

Distinguishing your true stories from the ones that aren't true for you protects you from the seven billion people who want to keep you in line.

6 You Have the Right to Take Your Time

Often people want answers *right now!* When they tell you to jump, they want you to ask, "How high?"

But you have the right to think things over. The right to delay. The right to say, "Okay, give me some time to see how I feel about it." The right to get to know the people who enter your life in either business or relationships and see if they are the right fit.

We spend most of each day in small or large negotiations with the people and environments around us. Often the best way to negotiate is to take the time and space to determine what is best for you. You succeed by saying yes only when you are ready and the conditions are right.

In removing yourself temporarily from the situation, you *reduce* the supply of yourself. In basic economics, value is a function of supply and demand. When supply goes down, value goes up.

A small delay so you can determine the best choice will likewise increase your value in any situation or relationship. But this is not really about getting something out of the situation, although it might have that effect. It is about allowing the necessary pause to notice what is actually happening and make decisions that come from a place of power in you, rather than rushing your decisions and making choices based on your preconditioning.

7 You Have the Right to Be Honest, Above All, with Yourself

You are entitled to say NO to wearing a mask in order to get people to like you. You can trust that the way you are is fine, that your honesty is what attracts others to you, and that your truth is what lights your internal fire.

The world right now is filled with fog. Honesty is a beacon. Your honesty—saying no to the lying—is what will bring the lost ships home. It's what will bring health, love, and money to you.

8 You Have the Right to an Abundant and Fulfilled Life

You are entitled to say NO to the scarcity complex, and any other complex, for that matter. You have the right to notice the fearful thoughts that do not belong to you, but rather simply pass through you—the ones that intend to scare you, cajole you, and keep you small—and to let them go, one at a time.

9 You Have the Right to Be Here Now

You are entitled to say NO to time traveling. Angers and regrets are in the past. Anxieties and worries are in the future. Traveling to the past or the future will not help you now. You have the right to say no to what is not happening right now. It will never solve your future problems but will always sap your present strengths.

10 You Have the Right to Silence

You are entitled to say NO to all the noise around you, to the news, to the responsibilities, to the pressures. You can sit alone in silence for a while, every day, to connect with the higher part of you, the part that wants to help you, and *let* it help you. You can be still for a moment, each day, and know that you are enough.

Out of stillness flows infinity.

11 You Have the Right to Surrender

You are entitled to surrender even the ideas you have formed about yourself. This is the ultimate No: saying NO to what you *think* you are.

It means that you surrender to the road. You reach out and trust that a loving hand will grab hold of you and guide you to take that first step.

There is nobody you need to impress. There is nobody who is judging you. And there will be nobody who can stop you.

One step at a time, the journey will take you where you need to go.

WHY THIS BOOK
IS FOR YOU

Just because you have picked up this book and are reading this page, we know some things about you.

You want to improve your life. You want to be happier. You want to add and remove some boundaries.

These might be physical boundaries, mental boundaries, emotional boundaries, or even spiritual boundaries. You want to remove blocks that you feel keep you from what life has to offer.

And you are a naturally giving person. Perhaps one who is more likely to say yes to those in need than no to those who simply ask too much.

What we show in this book is that No comes from a deep core inside. A spiritual core. One that allows you to tap into power you might not have known you had.

A power that can bring abundance into your life—incredible abundance. A power that can bring love into your life—the love you know you deserve. A power that will ultimately bring peace into your life when you say no to the noise and distractions that cling to all of us.

The Power of No has helped us, the authors, literally survive. With it, we have freed ourselves from the society, institutions, friends, loves, colleagues, bosses, and belief systems that tried to build a cage around us. Those that have tried and still try to control us.

Each No eliminates a cage. Each level of No we describe in this book sets us free. As humans, we are all entitled to find that freedom, whatever form it takes. Whatever form we want it to take.

And why not? Infinity existed before we were born. Infinity will exist after we leave this planet. Why not reach our full potential, unveil our mighty powers, during the small sliver of time we visit here?

Because you're reading this book, we know you are already very courageous. And you're ready for the final leap it takes to tap into your power.

This power has helped us keep negative influences out of our lives and make room for positive influences. To draw in money, love, health, and opportunity. When you take risks, you become unique; you stand out and can reach for the stars. No is a risk, but you are already brave enough to handle the Power of No.

It's important to ask the question "Should I say no?" in many different life circumstances. Thinking about this, wondering about it, debating it, pondering it, leads you to a deeper understanding of who you are, of what is good for you and your life and for the people around you. It ultimately leads you to situations where you can say yes to the abundance that was always meant for you.

After all, despite the title of this book, the ultimate goal is to say yes—to bring a blissful Yes into your life, one that opens the door to opportunities, abundance, and love.

Every day we are enchanted by what this new Yes has brought into our lives, and we know you will be also.

Rules for This Book

We want to make reading this book a pleasant experience for you. So right now we'll give you some guidelines on how it works.

There are two authors: James Altucher and Claudia Azula Altucher. When either of them is telling a personal story, she or he will say who is speaking.

When a chapter doesn't specify who is speaking, then both are speaking at the same time, often talking over each other until words finally spill out onto the page.

Hi! (from Claudia)

Hi! (from James)

Hi! (from both of us)

There is a method to the madness in the chapters, too.

There are seven levels of No.

They go from the very gross energies involved in protecting our bodies, our lives, and our basic boundaries to the more subtle energies that, when channeled well through the Power of No, bring about real love and compassion, to the highest levels of discrimination and wisdom that sprout from being exactly who we are.

At first we explore the everyday No's—the ones that might occur in relationships, or in jobs, or in your health, or when random space aliens shove you on the street (say no to them and then *run!*).

Then we start to find the No inside. Society uses our formative years to teach us all the things we are supposed to say yes to. Now we need to learn which ones it might be better to say no to. Society may have our best intentions at heart, but ultimately we are the ones choosing which kind of life we want to live.

It's not our parents' fault. Or our schools'. Or the government's. Or our friends'. They all have their own issues—no need to blame them. But there's no need to say yes to their stories either. Now is the time for us to build our own stories.

We conclude by looking at the No that is deep inside. The silence. The core from which wisdom flows. When we dig the well that reaches that wisdom, we can drink forever.

That's the No that brings real power.

When you reach that flow, that's when you can say yes! and know that you are coming from a place of self-wisdom. That's when you say yes! in a balanced way, from the heart.

Here's a guideline to think about while reading this book:

a) Reading this book is good.

b) Thinking about it afterward is 100 times better.

c) Practicing what it says is 100,000 times better.

Learning to say no in many areas of your life is very difficult—it takes a lot of practice. So in many of the chapters we provide exercises. What you read here will only help if you follow them. It is a daily practice of awareness that brings you into your own power.

You won't find exercises in every chapter. After all, part of the idea here is to get rid of the clutter in your life, to clean out the spaces so that silence and power can enter. With that in mind, we don't want to give you too much work to do. We added exercises where we felt they would be most useful.

It's good to have exercises to practice when necessary. We know because whenever we forget to say no there are consequences. And it's much better to practice acknowledging your feelings, taking a step back, reflecting, and wondering about the Power of No than to experience those consequences.

Always remember: It's one thing to say no. It's another thing to have the Power of No.

The Second Most
Powerful Word

JAMES: We all make mistakes that we regret later on. We quit one job for a worse one. We buy a house and then sell it at a loss. We lose a lot of money.

We cheat on or betray our spouses in some way and then lose family, children, and assets, and we end up lonely and starved for affection. Or, even worse, *we* are betrayed.

We eat unhealthy foods and end up with digestive problems. Of course, we now know that these first problems get much worse as we age: cancer, Alzheimer's, diabetes, and so on.

We spend time with people who don't inspire us.

One time someone wrote to us: "I'm applying all of the things you suggest, and I am coming up with a ton of ideas to improve my life. The only problem is, when I go out drinking with my friends on Friday night, they all laugh at the ideas. What should I do?"

We wrote back: "Simple solution: stay home on Friday night."

We never heard from him again.

But these aren't mistakes worth regretting. This is what it means to be human. Being human is very difficult.

The hardest thing we've ever had to do is be born. From that moment on, we are hungry. We are hungry not only for food but for experience, for pleasure, for many things that can't be given to us. Ever. Yet we stay hungry for them.

Sometimes it seems like everyone is smiling and happy, and we wonder how they can fake it so much. Those smiles seem like etches on a plastic mask. We can't believe they are real.

We live in a dream we've created. And when we say "we," we are talking about the authors of this book. How many times in the past have we wished for more but been afraid to tell people?

How many times were we afraid people would think we weren't perfect if we showed our true selves? How many times did we limit ourselves because we were afraid we would miss out on opportunities if anyone knew who we really were? How many times did we end up on the floor instead?

This is the mistake we often made. And this is how the authors of this book met each other. We are proud to say it.

We were both on the floor. Lives ruined. Not just our own but those of everyone around us.

We didn't know each other. We had no idea the other existed. But we both said it around the same time. A single word. The word that changed everything. We knew we couldn't handle it anymore. That it was our best thinking that got us here on the floor. We knew that whether it was to a friend, a colleague, a random person on the street, a divine presence, a subconscious—we had to say one word that would get us up off the floor and on the journey toward discovering the Power of No.

We had to say it and we did, and we hope you do also. It's a word that leads to gratitude, compassion, abundance, love, surrender, and *life*.

Help.

Once Upon a Time . . .

CLAUDIA: Once upon a time, when I was a very young girl, my aunt Meldy asked me a question that stopped me cold on my feet. I think I even stopped breathing: "Who do you like best, your aunt Marta or me?"

I remember the sudden stop, the tension permeating everything, mostly because the adults stopped talking. They all looked at me. What would this little girl say to such an important question?!

And because I was not moving like I usually did, like running into the bathroom to fire up the blow dryer, and then back to the kitchen to open the refrigerator, and back to the bathroom to get rollers in my hair, and so on, I could pause.

I was a tornado. And sometimes a tornado needs to slow down and take a deep breath.

I considered the question. Even at six, I knew it was tricky. Feelings were involved. But I told the truth.

"Marta," I said. Marta had always loved me. But she also always stopped me from hurting myself. She wanted to protect me. Just like right now the universe wants to protect us if we give it a chance. If we listen.

The adults were silent, still looking at me. That is when I said: "Because sometimes she says no."

— FIRST —

THE NO THAT CHOOSES LIFE

*You have the right to defend
and live your life . . .*

CLAUDIA: "I want to die" is the most popular Google search phrase to reach James's blog. Horrible, isn't it? And then again, is it?

Over many years of just living, I have come to realize that nobody has it easy. Anyone over the age of two, maybe earlier even, can already speak of hardships. *Mommy left for the supermarket, and I felt she would abandon me forever . . . I'm not as popular because of my braces and people sharing horrible photos of me on Instagram . . . I'm divorced and broke and very scared now.*

Sometimes these hardships are more than we can bear. Often they are divinely sent wake-up calls pointing to what needs to go so we can come back to ourselves.

Whenever I've found myself reaching for those four words, *I want to die,* it's not physical death I am craving but a different type. What I've wanted, again and again, has been the death of the old ways, the death of behaviors and patterns of thinking that no longer serve me, the attitudes and responses that keep me going in circles and stuck. I have wanted the death of what has to die within me so I can find a new life.

Many times this has involved acknowledging that killing myself was not the answer. This is a lesson I learned very early on, but it still did not stop me—or James—from trying.

Spirit wants to teach us whatever it is we came here to learn.

When we see it this way, we find meaning. Suffering is transformed. We are ready to listen and act on the things we can control.

We are ready to live.

How the Power of No
Saved My Physical Life

JAMES: When I was at my lowest, when everything had disappeared, I considered suicide.

I heard a story once: If you put three cigarettes in a glass of water, the pure nicotine will leach into the water overnight. Then if you drink the water in the morning you will be dead within 60 seconds from a heart attack.

Then my kids could at least get life insurance. Then maybe the world would be better.

I had no more desire to survive.

It was three in the morning, the time when nightmares laugh side by side with reality.

One of my little girls got up and wandered into the room I was sitting in. "Daddy," she said, "I'm having a bad dream."

"Go back to sleep, honey."

"I can't. I'm afraid to."

"Count a hundred sheep."

She was wiping her eyes. "That never works," she said.

"Try this technique," I told her. "Instead of sheep, list a hundred things you are grateful for. That's always a nice way to fall asleep."

"Okay," she said and went back to her room.

I took a deep breath. I also started to list the things I was grateful for.

Being grateful is the bridge between the world of nightmares and the world where we are free to say no. It's the bridge between the world of delusions and the world of creativity.

It's the power that brings death back to life, the power that turns poverty to wealth and anger to compassion.

I said no to killing myself.

I am still alive.

SAVE YOUR LIFE

If you find yourself in danger of taking your own life, I urge you to stop everything now and do the necessary thing: ask for help. Find another person and say out loud to him or her: "I need your help because I am thinking of harming myself."

Do it now, because it is impossible for you to see things clearly when you are alone and in the throes of a mental attack of anger turned inward.

It is not a sign of weakness; it is actually the bravest thing you can do.

If you are not at risk, if you are grounded within your life and ready to continue the journey, then gratitude has a way of getting you out of your head and back into the flow. It reminds you how full of abundance you already are.

Do this: Every day this week, write an e-mail to people who have done you a favor at some point. Tell them why you are writing to them.

Do not expect a response, but document the letters and any responses in a diary.

Believe it or not, this is not only a spiritual practice but an abundance practice as well. Abundance and spirituality go hand in hand.

When you have abundance, you become the infinite well others can drink from. When you are spiritual, the universe rewards you with its favors. The two are intertwined.

In the third level of No, we explore more ways to completely reinvent yourself. But the e-mail challenge helps you acknowledge the good people in your life and easily recognize who to say yes to and who to say no to. Often this is the first step.

How the Power of No
Saved My Emotional Life

JAMES: The first girl I dated after separating from my first wife asked me what my net worth was, half an hour after we met.

I was honest, and I told her. She said, "That's not enough."

Another time I asked her, "How come you never introduce me to your friends?"

She said, "Because you're too crazy."

That made a lot of sense. I do not introduce my crazy friends to my normal friends. One of her friends was running for the senate or for governor or something. It would've created a lot of problems if he was seen hanging out with a crazy person. But I could've maybe offered to be vice president if he ever made it that far.

One time she said to me, "My people can destroy your people."

I doubt it. My people at that time were largely zombies. In the movies you often see the governor totally powerless against the zombie army.

But I couldn't tell her that and reveal my true identity.

We broke up. I'd like to think I broke up with her, if it wasn't for that one conversation where she called me and said, "I'm not ready for you. I need time. A *lot* of time."

And then I broke up with her.

I was in a Borders bookstore at that moment, and she was at President Obama's first inauguration, and I still had a BlackBerry.

Those big buttons that required the slightest of pushes. We were texting. I remember typing out, "b . . . r . . . e . . . k" and then backspacing. You know the drill. I miss my BlackBerry.

Back then just a sliver of Chinese food could cause enlightenment. People were having orgasms over politics, and the country was heading toward the Apocalypse.

Nothing seemed to matter to me except being lonely, eating hot dogs for breakfast, being scared of going broke, and wandering around bookstores looking for someone to spend time with me.

I was losing my family. I had lost my job. I lost my house. I had lost millions of dollars, gained them back, lost them again, and so on.

That is when a window that was dirty, foggy, cracked, and iced suddenly cleared for me. I was already dead. I had to say no to the life I had created for myself since birth. That life simply hadn't worked.

I started to say no to people who weren't right for me. I started to say no to everything I didn't want to do.

When you have a tiny, tiny piece of crap in your soup, it doesn't matter how much more water you pour in and how many more spices you put on top. There's crap in your soup.

I had been saying yes to the wrong things for 20 years.

Within six months my life was completely different. I met Claudia. I moved into a half-decent apartment. I was working on ideas that actually made money. And I needed fewer and fewer things to make me happy. That's true minimalism. That's the Power of No.

Every six months since then my life has transformed. Even in the past few days as I write, remarkable things have happened. I've interviewed Wayne Dyer for my show, for example. Sometimes I wonder, *How did something that remarkable happen?* He doesn't give that many interviews, after all, and he had not heard of me before then.

When you start saying no to bad things, the Yeses compound every day. Yeses compound automatically, the way interest does in a bank.

You may think it is not possible to say no to a situation in which lots of other people are involved, or a dysfunctional job, or a dysfunctional family. I propose you hear me out and keep reading. There is always a way. It might not be immediate, but it can be done.

When that woman asked me what my net worth was, I could've just said no and gotten up and not wasted three months of my life. But as easy as that sounds, I didn't know how to do it.

Now I do. Now I'm free. I dumped the old soup. Now I can finally drink from the soup I just cooked.

Saying No to an Untimely Death

JAMES: Often we are given recipes for "success" to get "motivated!" to find "purpose!"

Make your to-do lists! Do this! Do that! Take these pills, and call us in the morning!

The antiaging industry is like that. There's a big list of things to do if you want to live longer. We don't want to give you more things to do.

Sometimes it's important to *not* do more things, even if you think those things will improve your life. We're all busy people already. Who needs the stress of doing more? Sometimes it's important to do less in order to attract abundance.

But it is important to try to live longer so you have more time to practice the things we tell you in this book!

There's a very simple trick to living longer. And it doesn't involve doing *more* things. We almost feel silly telling you this: don't do things that will cause you to die.

That's it. Postpone dying. At least to the extent you can control.

Okay, let's dig a little deeper into that. And as we dig deeper you will see this is an example that can be applied to many areas of your life.

If you go to CDC.gov (the Centers for Disease Control and Prevention) you can see what the top causes of death were last year.

Here's the top ten:

1. Heart disease

2. Cancer

3. Chronic lower respiratory diseases

4. Stroke (cerebrovascular diseases)

5. Accidents (unintentional injuries)

6. Alzheimer's disease

7. Diabetes

8. Nephritis, nephrotic syndrome, and nephrosis

9. Influenza and pneumonia

10. Intentional self-harm (suicide)

This is great information. Maybe your grandparents died of heart disease. So it might be in your family. Wouldn't it be great to avoid heart disease?

Does that mean you should drink wine? Or take some sort of blood thinning (or thickening) pill? Or get an operation?

No. It means you can choose to say no to the things that *cause* heart disease.

- Smoking

- High blood pressure (work on ways to reduce stress and anger)

- Sedentary lifestyle (Take a 10-minute walk a day. Take breaks in your work every 40 minutes)

- Poor diet (Okay, maybe eat some vegetables. Or better yet, drink your vegetables)

- Obesity

- Excessive alcohol use

- Too much salt

That's it. Now if you have a history of heart disease in your family and you just say no to all those things, you will live longer than you would've otherwise lived.

Maybe it's hard to say no to all of these things at once. Okay— just pick one. Then later on, you can pick two.

Thank the authors later.

The same can apply to anything. Think of something important to you. Money. Your marriage. Your relationships with your children or friends.

Many people ask, "How can I meet the woman (or man) of my dreams?"

We have no idea! Maybe your dreams are nightmares.

Make a list of the things you are doing where you can avoid your worst nightmares. Start with that.

— EXERCISE —
SAY NO TO STRESS

Sometimes we need rest and proper boundaries. Sometimes we need to do less. When we forget that we have rhythms and cycles just like nature does (because we are nature), we force things, overwork, burn the candle at both ends, and make poor choices as a consequence of exhaustion.

This exercise offers ways to protect your inner happy place, the wise source from which all decisions are made.

Pick something *very* important to you. It can be anything: your art, sex, your relationship to your community, your job, for example. Make a list of the things to say no to in order to improve that part of your life.

For example, keeping your level of stress down is very important, so here are five things we can think of to say no to so that you can have centered and relaxed days:

1. Say no to anything that gets in the way of your daily practices, no matter how IMPORTANT it pretends to be.

2. Say no to anything that prevents you from sitting in silence for some time, every day.

3. Never watch the news, on TV or on the Internet (you are what you mentally "eat").

4. Do not talk to people who you know do not respect you or who put you down.

5. Don't argue with people. It's okay to say, "You're right" if it means saving time and energy.

Thinking of energy in these terms helps us to recognize where we need to draw the line and where we need to ask for help.

Saying No to Negative Chatter

The Power of No happens from the core of your being.

- You need *discernment* (to know how to see the fabric of myths in your life).

- You need *compassion* (to know when your power could cause harm to others).

- You need *health* (to have the energy to create the life you want to live).

Most people love, or try to love, their kids, their spouses, and their friends. Most people try to take care of the ones they love and be there for them.

But sometimes we get stuck. Our obligations run up against true longings that come from deep inside. Longings that can't be ignored.

We get stuck in negative chatter that becomes a running commentary on our lives, much like a news anchor who only tells us the bad news that happens all day long.

Examples of negative chatter: "How could he do this to me?" "Why does that person look like an idiot?" "Do I look ugly?"

"How am I going to survive my job today?" "Am I going to be able to pay the bills?" And on and on.

Throughout the day we get filled with doubts. Maybe some people don't. But the authors, Claudia and James, often do.

We think of people from our past who have done us wrong, and we get angry. We might even obsess about this anger.

Or we worry about some upcoming event, and we get afraid.

It's a practice for many of us not to be filled with self-doubt and anxiety all day long.

Often we beat ourselves up in ways in which we would never beat up someone we loved. This is the worst form of cruelty. It's a daily practice to recognize when this is happening and then to say to ourselves, "I am here for you, honey. I love you and want to take care of you."

THE THREE KEYS TO STOP NEGATIVE CHATTER

The first key is to catch yourself when you are starting to feel "the anger." Anger *never* accomplishes what you want it to.

The second key is to treat yourself like someone you love. And "fake it till you make it" if you can't. Imagine someone you love. Imagine what you would say to him or her. Now say it to yourself.

Cradle yourself like a mother cradles her baby.

The third key is to treat others with love. Without the first and the second key to show you how, this is much more difficult.

But it's important. Do you stay with the anger, or do you practice compassion? It's your choice, but we hope you choose compassion.

WE DO THESE EXERCISES BECAUSE . . .

The reason for all of these exercises and all of these ways of looking at real change in our lives is that change is difficult.

We've spent a lifetime being programmed about what is "right" and what is "wrong." Now we're opening ourselves up to new ways of looking at things.

These methods let enormous power enter our lives so we can manifest real change.

All of these methods are designed specifically to let the abundance in. To let wealth in. To let love and creativity in.

All of these start with *trust*. Trust that you are reading this book for a reason.

What Do You Do When You Hit Bottom?

JAMES: I sold my first business for a lot of money. This became my worst nightmare. In the early 2000s my company built websites for entertainment companies. Bad Boy Records, Miramax, Time Warner, HBO, Sony, Disney, Loud Records, Interscope, and on and on. Oh, and Con Edison.

Then I saw that kids in junior high school were learning HTML, so I sold the business.

I bought an apartment for millions. I rebuilt it. Feng shui! I bought art. I played a lot of poker. I began investing in companies—a million here, a few hundred thousand there.

Then I started more companies. Then I bought more things. Then I became an addict—the worst kind of addict.

From June 2000 until September 2001, I probably lost $1 million a week.

I couldn't stop. I wanted to get back up to the peak. I wanted to be loved. I wanted to have $100 million so people would love me.

I lived with so much regret. There was so much good I could've done. But I wasted it.

And when I regretted, I would "time travel" away from the present, reliving the past over and over again.

I felt like I was going to die. That zero equals death. I couldn't believe how stupid I had been. I lost all my friends. Nobody returned calls. I went to the ATM machine—there was $143 left.

There were no jobs; there was nothing.

One weekend when I had $0 left in my bank account I called my parents to borrow money, but they said no. That was the last time I spoke to my dad, who had a stroke six months later and then died.

I tried meditation to calm down, but it didn't work. There was too much anxiety in my head. I never slept. I lost 30 pounds. I'm five feet nine, and I went from 160 to 130. I couldn't talk to anyone. I couldn't move. I stopped having ideas. I cried every day.

There was never a moment when I didn't feel sick. I had let my kids down. I would die, and they would never remember me.

My then-wife, the kids, and I moved 80 miles north of NYC with the tiny bit of money we took out of our apartment after being forced to sell at a loss. I couldn't leave the house for three months. I was depressed. I gained back all my weight and then another 30 pounds. Finally I had to either die or feed my family. I was forced to choose myself.

But first, I had to get grounded.

It wasn't a sudden realization. It wasn't that suddenly I had nothing to lose so I was infinitely happy. You can't go from lying on the floor to flying in the sky. Maybe some can. But I couldn't.

I had to start with the basics. I had to exercise the basic muscles of a healthy life: physically, emotionally, mentally, and spiritually. I had to do this for my own self-interest. But making myself healthy was also the best effort I could make for the people around me, the people I loved.

— EXERCISE —
THE DAILY PRACTICE
TO GET OFF THE FLOOR

JAMES: We never come out of desperation and pain in just one single act. It's not "magic." Living is a day-to-day thing, and so is the practice of returning from depression, or picking ourselves up off the floor, or beginning the journey back from dark places.

This Daily Practice is what has worked for me again and again on my journey back from the dark nights of my life. It continues to change my life for the better every six months, and it guarantees I will fall back into depression if I forget it.

This is what I did:

- I started to exercise every day. I started to eat better. One item for breakfast. A healthy lunch. Tiny dinner. No snacks.

- I started to sleep nine hours a night. More on this later.

- I started to be around only people who loved and supported me. I broke off all ties with anyone it felt bad to be around.

- I wrote down ideas every day for articles I could write and businesses I could start. Bit by bit I started to get paid to write. If you don't exercise the idea muscle, it atrophies just like any other muscle. And it atrophies quickly. You *must* work the idea muscle every day to turn into an idea machine.

The Power of No

- I decided I wanted to help people and be honest every day. I was grateful for my daughters. I was grateful for what I had. I didn't fight reality or regret. This was my reality and I had to make the best of it.

- I had to learn surrender. If an athlete comes to the race prepared and does the best he can, he is a true professional and he can surrender to the results. I had to surrender to the fact that I couldn't control everything. But I could be prepared.

- Every day I came to the game prepared.

And life got better. I became an idea machine. I started businesses. I sold businesses. I started writing and got millions of readers. Life got good.

Then I stopped using the fundamental techniques I just described. I was really bad; I did everything you should not do. I was like an addict. Picture the worst abuses. That was me. Again.

And then I lost it all again. Everything. Agh! I had to start over. I couldn't even believe I had to start from scratch.

Every time I've lost money and love, it's because I squandered my physical, emotional, mental, and spiritual health. Now, every day without fail, I do the Daily Practice to exercise the basic muscles of a healthy life. And it's worked. I hope. I pray I don't squander it again.

Often you hear it's not about the end; it's about the journey. This is not true. It's not about the journey, and it never was. It's about right now. It's about choosing to be healthy in those four areas right now and saying no to everything that blocks that.

Right now is the only place you'll ever be. Choose not to waste it.

SECOND

THE NO THAT BRINGS TRUE LOVE, CREATIVITY, AND ABUNDANCE

*You have the right to real
and supportive love, to soar in your
creativity, and to fly in abundance . . .*

Why do sex and love appear so early in a book about saying no?

It's a fair question, and here's another for you: how do sex and love relate to abundance and creativity? To put it simply, being clear about which relationships and which people we let into our lives is the key to access our creative forces.

When it comes to sex and the "idea" of what love might be—likely based on Hollywood movies—all of us have huge potential to derail brutally from the tracks of our creative life train and crash into a dark psychological place from which it might take us years to return.

When it comes to sex and love, we run the risk of becoming people we don't recognize: actors instead of real people. We change in order to please, put on airs to become breathtaking, or exaggerate to impress.

When our No's are not in place, we are vulnerable to abuse. Vulnerability opens a door, and the mean forces of perdition have an entry—and they will take it.

This is okay. In many cases, we simply never learned how to love. Or we followed the wrong examples or had the wrong teachers.

But if our No's are not in place here, whenever we get angry or hurt and go unconscious, we immediately seek the next thrill to distract us, dull us, and numb us.

Sex is a great distraction, and "love" relationships created for the wrong reasons can seem like a wonderful substitute. Hey! We look good on paper.

Filtering the people we allow into our lives is probably the most important factor in determining whether we will live a happy life or not. Because if we let the wrong people in, we will be drained, and if we are drained, how can we expect to have abundance or creativity?

It just does not add up.

If we have crappy people around, we have a crappy life. If we have supportive, encouraging people around, we have a creative and abundant life. The people who bring pain are the same people who drain. Don't let them take your beautiful energy. We do not say this for poetic flair—this is a plea. Please don't let the people who pull you down remain in your life.

We have seen men lose businesses, families, and inheritances over an inability to stop paying prostitutes and buying expensive cars and showing off. We've seen marriages happen on the spur of the moment only to be dissolved a week later even though the energy was so right at that one special moment. We've seen women stay in abusive marriages for the wrong reasons (money, a false sense of security, a house) and die because of it, literally.

Reconsider who you call your friends, lovers, and partners. You could be surprised. Because if you don't say no to crappy people, your life will go down the drain.

WHO IS YOUR INNER CIRCLE?

List all of the primary people in your life: family, friends, co-workers, neighbors. Anyone you engage with more than five times a week.

Rate on a scale of 1 to 10 how you feel after your interactions with that person, 10 being the best.

Anyone lower than an 8, begin to pull back from. Lower than a 5, stay a little farther away from.

If you see them at work, nod your head and say hello but limit engagement.

Be a surgeon. You are operating on all of your social relationships. It doesn't matter: boss, family, colleagues, anyone. This doesn't mean being selfish and avoiding people who need your help. You can be there for them. But put the oxygen mask on your own face first when the plane makes an emergency landing.

Also, it doesn't mean you cut people off completely if they rate low on your list. This is a dimmer switch, not an on-and-off switch. It is a tool for being discriminating so you can bring your brightest creativity forward.

Saying No to People You Know Are Not Good for You

CLAUDIA: In the autumn of 2002 I fell in love with Tim. At least that's what I told myself as I walked out of the bookstore floating on air.

To be fair, what I really did was project all the qualities I wished I had onto him, and then loved him for them. Funny, it's so easy to go unconscious when it comes to romantic relationships.

He was a piano virtuoso. He had talent, and he had money.

I had a job I hated and nothing to show for my own creativity. My own talents were deeply buried within my fears of daring to create anything. Oh, and I was broke.

On our second date he took me to his studio and, just for me, played one of Liszt's most romantic compositions: *Liebestraum,* which, adding insult to injury, means "dream of love" in German.

As Tim played, my jaw dropped and then electricity started to mount; tingles of sensation popped all over my body—electric addiction. At times my eyes closed involuntarily. Delusion was getting me drunk.

He was *the one.*

I knew nothing about him. But I knew he was the one.

And just like that, I was swept up into the tornado of love addiction. It was intoxicating. I was intrigued, I craved more. I wanted to marry him. He, naturally, took the opportunity to have me.

After the private piano recital he didn't call me back for six months. But when he finally did I was excited.

Never mind the half year of total unexplained absence. I *loved* him. Why didn't my few friends understand this? Maybe it was because I had not told anyone. I wanted to surprise everyone with the wedding. In my mind it was all working out.

I couldn't believe it when, after what was now our third date, he didn't call back the next day, or the next. I tried calling, but there was never an answer.

Months went by again. I told myself he was probably busy, shy, traveling.

Around the third time he called, I told a friend that I couldn't resist him, that he had power over me.

She said he had no power over me. I was the one giving power away. I was the one saying yes when I needed to say no.

I went out with him again. And I ate at the restaurant, and I smelled the flowers, and I heard the hints of promises to come.

And I knew it was all wrong. But still, I gave him the gun and permission to execute me. Or at least my sense of self-worth. I died a little that night.

I went down knowing. I wasn't a victim at all; I was a full participant.

The next day I was miserable. I knew I wanted out. Every time you die a little, you're that much closer to being left for dead.

I wanted out not only because this hurt me but also because now I wanted the real thing. I wanted love, a partner, a friend, someone who would love me and whom I would love back. I did not want leftovers.

When you're left for dead you have to find a new life in order to survive.

So finally it hit me. Finally I knew what to do.

Then he called again.

"Hi Tim, how can I help you?" I said. I was shaking.

"'How can I hee-elp you?'" he said, mocking me.

I did not bite. I took a deep breath.

"What part of *I don't ever want to talk to you again* don't you understand?" I said.

I had never said those words to him before, but he did understand. We had seen each other four times over a period of two years. He wasn't stupid. He had once told me he was "Ivy League."

He attempted to justify himself: "What happened was that . . ."

This was my chance to turn my No into my law. This is where the No of sex counts; this is where we take our self-worth back, and with it, our energy, our desire to create. This is the moment to own our talent and to stand for what we are: magnificent creatures.

"I'm hanging up now," I said. And I did.

I felt terrible; my stomach was in a knot. Owning our self-worth can feel like that at first. It might be a new sensation, but by God it pays off.

If it's good for you, then it is God for you.

Back then, I still wondered: *Did I do the right thing? Will I ever be as interesting as I was when I was with him? What if this was finally going to be the time when he meant it?*

But I now know three things:

1. If he doesn't mean it the first time, he doesn't mean it at all. Period.

2. To attract the coolest man, I had to become the coolest woman—and this is not just in love; it is in every aspect of life.

3. To become the coolest woman, I had to realize I was worth it, uncover my own creative talent, and use it.

You will never find your own creative talent by saying yes to all of the people who seek to drain you with relationships that go nowhere, or people who try to control you or put you down, or people who cheat you or lie to you.

In this area it is pretty black and white: either you are

supported by those around you, or you are dragged into the spiral drain of the toilet, and off you go to some sewer.

Recently, years after this Tim incident, I was editing a video of myself doing a yoga backbend. This is one of my many creative projects. Just then, through my headphones, I heard *Liebestraum* play.

Watching a video of my own talent to the tune of the same music that once drained me felt like coming to a universal agreement. I interpreted it as a "Well done!" No. A nod from God whispering into my ears: "Shine your own light now. You go, girl!" This is the No of rising like a phoenix from the ashes of addiction and delusion.

It is the No of harnessing our sexual energy so we can create life in any form—relationships, babies, art. Whatever our heart desires.

It is saying No to cheap drama.

Thank God I am writing this instead of waiting for a call.

(James: Amen!)

—— EXERCISE ——
WHERE DID MY CREATIVITY GO?

Do you feel that there is a creative side to you that has gone underground? What did you love doing as a child that you no longer do? It might be reading or drawing or writing or singing. Choose anything that makes you feel like time does not exist and you are in the flow.

First, write these things down on a piece of paper. For example: I like to draw, to interpret my dreams, to have time for reflection, to read books that have deep meaning, to look at old comic books.

Keep these notes near your computer.

Let them be there as part of your life.

Let them return to your life by keeping your awareness on them.

Saying No for Love

CLAUDIA: *Give me the death I must have!* I prayed. And death, believe me, I received.

I prayed those words while looking at the chipped paint ceiling of the South Indian house I was renting with four other people. I prayed to the energies of transformation. To whatever God might be listening.

My prayer was simple. I wanted to never have to feel the pain I was about to inflict on myself. Again.

I had met Bill in Mysore during a yoga intensive trip. On our first date, which I initiated, I delighted in his conversation, but underneath it all I was planning our wedding. (Maybe you notice a pattern here; this was only a few years after Tim.)

On our second date I took him downtown. I dressed in red. He had agreed to spend the whole day with me. Everything was going my way.

During lunch I seized the opportunity to ask him what he thought about love. He looked uncomfortable and gave me a yoga scripture type of explanation: "Love is universal."

"No," I said, "what do you think about man-woman? About relationships? About *love?*" It didn't remotely occur to me that I had just met Bill and that this was a highly personal question. I wanted him to say what I wanted to hear, and I wanted it now. He dodged the question. Good for him.

Finally the time came for our third and last date. I was to board a plane that would take me back home that evening. He would return to Canada a few weeks later.

I don't know what I was thinking as I put on makeup to go out with him. Delusion has a way of blurring things and making up almost-coherent stories that cover up the coldest of realities. I thought I was to get my Sleeping Beauty wake-up kiss that evening. What I got instead was the death I had asked for.

He didn't know it was Valentine's Day until we walked into the Domino's Pizza and saw all the heart balloons floating around.

Toward the end of the date, when no attempt at kissing came around, instead of the delusion I started to feel despair. Bill was going to break me into a million pieces. Something had gone wrong with me. Again.

Again!

Later that evening while packing, I started to cry.

Back home in New Jersey I was upset when I didn't hear from him. My fantasies of moving to Canada faded, and I began to feel angry, tense, upset, and like a complete failure. Why did I find myself in the same black hole I thought I had escaped the last time, with Tim?

What was wrong with me?

Since all of my energy had been spent pursuing unavailable men, I was depleted and lacking creativity. One night I was reading Julia Cameron's *The Artist's Way*, looking for inspiration. In it, she writes that the chapter on withdrawal from *Sex and Love Addicts Anonymous* should be mandatory reading for everyone.

That was the first time love and addiction had appeared in my mind in the same sentence. My eyes lifted from the book. Could it be?

Could it be that maybe all this pursuing of men who never loved me back, and this relentless desire to control the outcome of relationships, had something to do with addiction? I had to at least find out. I located a support group near me. Maybe death had something to do with embarrassing myself in front of strangers.

One night, in the clumsiest way, filled with embarrassment and with tears in my eyes, I admitted my vulnerabilities to a group of people sitting in a circle. I told them of my uncanny ability to find and pursue unavailable men until I made them run away.

This small act of vulnerability, which did feel like a complete death to me, turned out to be the lifesaver I needed. It saved me to know I was not alone. It taught me that death has a lot less to do with funerals and a lot more to do with daring to do the most courageous thing ever: ask for help, even when it feels like we are exposing our hearts.

Fast forward: My friend Gary has never been to a love addiction gathering; he has never sought help. One afternoon last summer he told me that the night before he had gone on a date with a woman, Lisa. At the beginning of their date, he said something mean to her so he would have an advantage. She, of course, counteracted by following some strategies of her own, to gain back control.

When things started going differently than Gary had planned, he said he had to leave, because he was a busy man. Within ten minutes they were making out in the lobby of her hotel, he told me. He was proud. Had he won?

Nobody had won that night, because nobody had been on that date that night. As far as I could see, two bodies were out and about in Orlando, but no souls. Gary and Lisa were not there; rather, it was two sets of rules playing against each other, two books filled with instructions, pick-up lines, controlling strategies, and a ten-step guide for making a swift exit when it all goes wrong.

The actual Gary and Lisa were left behind, in their hotel rooms, lonely, hoping for love, feeling sad and undeserving, wondering why this was all happening again.

I understand what happened to Gary. I am, after all, something akin to the world champion of trying to control relationships. I did that until the age of 40.

The death I asked for—and got—that night was to realize that at the time, much like Gary, I had never been present on a date either. I had never met a man without having an agenda, without a plan. I was never there. Instead, a dictated set of "instructions" and "rules" and long-term "plans" went to the date in my place. A robot programmed by a fallible programmer—me. I had been following rules and regulations that I overheard others talk about. I bought into the lie that if I followed certain steps, anything other than my own truth, I would be guaranteed happiness. It never worked.

After Julia Cameron's suggestion, I read the chapter she mentioned, and I went to a meeting. I am Claudia, I said, and I think I am a love addict.

The death I asked for and needed was to acknowledge that I was addicted. To acknowledge that I was sabotaging myself by playing a game dictated by other people's rules. By what others thought would work. By processes that so-called experts work hard to perfect so that you will have the perfect date, only you will not be on it, or anywhere near it. The rules will.

The death I needed was to realize that I am not in control of anything, especially when it comes to relationships. I can't control a man any more than I can control what my brother will say or do, or what my now husband will publish on Facebook (James: well, she can occasionally control that). Or what a boss will do. Or what a bank will do. And on and on, all the myths we fight for fruitlessly.

The death I needed was to say no to my relentless obsession to orchestrate every relationship.

When I finally admitted that my best thinking had gotten me to being 40, single, and lonely, what happened was completely different from what I thought would happen. Suddenly, and to my surprise, I had help. There were others in the hole with me, trying to figure it out together, listening to each other, showing me that men had feelings, too, just like women.

Death wasn't so bad. In fact it seemed to come bearing gifts. Months after attending these meetings, many of us started going to dances together. Nobody dated anybody because we were all "sober," and we knew that if we felt inclined to date someone in the group we would have to talk about it, in the open, in front of everybody. We knew that being vulnerable and talking about what our tendencies were was the only way to accept them, run reality checks on them, correct them, and heal.

Now I was part of a pack that, for better or worse, was all together in the same mess. I had a support group of other humans who, just like me, had been under the illusion of control for so long. Perhaps out of exhaustion, we were finally ready to get honest.

The paths that had taken us to this place were different. Some were anorexic in love, meaning that they could not accept love and lived in fantasies instead. Some spent all evenings and weekends watching pornography; others pursued unavailable people and stalked them, or planned weddings on first dates: yes, that would have been me.

But all of us had one thing in common: we were tired of it. We wanted to change, and we wanted real partners who would have our backs.

And when we admitted it, we found each other. When we admitted it, it was as if God opened the doors and said, "Finally! Please come on in. I've been waiting for you, and now I can finally help you. I am so glad to see you."

We had all thought that we could tamper with the most powerful energy we have as humans—that of sex, which leads to birth, to evolution, and to death.

How deluded was I to think that I could control or manipulate *that* energy? How crazy was I to think that this force could be dominated by human-made rules and strategies, or to believe, even for a second, that I owned it?

When I found this group I was caught in a vicious cycle of arrogance and denial, thinking I could tap into this source of life all by myself, without help, without prayer, and without respect for it, using only my limited mind and understanding for my own pleasure. That was my "best" thinking.

It wasn't that we were out of our minds; it was that we were too far *into* our minds. We were trapped by them. We were caught in endless threads of "she said, he said," and "if I do this, then he will probably think that," and "if I put her down, then she will sleep with me and want me even more." We thought this could prevent us from feeling the vulnerability of real love. Protect us from being who we were.

Taking the step of admitting that I was powerless over this addiction was a scary thing to do because I risked being a loser. A loser according to every convention I had previously held to be true.

In the end the courage to risk it paid off because when I did touch bottom and admit to myself and others that I needed help, it felt as if my eyes finally opened. And I saw light at the end of the tunnel.

As I went to support group meetings I noticed the things that had been holding me back: Deep-seated grief that needed to be either forgiven or let go. Wrongdoings that I needed to come to terms with.

I started to heal. Discernment grew in me, and so did sobriety. One step at a time, one day at a time.

—→ EXERCISE →—

WE ARE THE AVERAGE OF THE FIVE PEOPLE WE SPEND TIME WITH

We often are the average of the five people we spend the most time with.

- Who are five people you spend time with in your life who inspire you? List them.

- Are these people you can trust? Are these people you listen to?

- Are these people with whom you can be yourself?

- Are these people who respect your need for space and boundaries?

- Organize times with these people when you can speak and listen to each other.

- Then the hard part: listen to them.

As you reflect on this, you may want to take it one step further. You are also the average of the five things you have around you, the ideas of the five books you have your attention on, the feelings from the five movies or shows you watch, and so on. Your immediate environment has a much deeper effect on you than you might think.

A Big Secret to Fulfill Your Desires

CLAUDIA: After sitting in a support group circle for a while, I regained sobriety. I did not pursue unavailable men anymore. In fact, I politely moved out of their way whenever I saw them.

Starting with No, following that with asking for help, together with support and increasing self-awareness, led me to *discernment,* and then to rediscovery of who I was and what I was capable of.

In March 2009 as I was sitting in one of these circles, my turn came to share for three minutes, and I told the group that since I knew I could reach God through their ears, I had an important message. I asked them to please listen closely.

I then addressed God and all the people present and told them that I was ready for a real relationship, one in which we would love, honor, and respect each other, one in which man and woman would be joined by a power greater than ourselves and in the service of that power.

I said I was ready for a relationship in which both parties would protect and love each other, but also protect and help the world in any way we were guided to.

I told the group that with those words I was also letting go of any attachment to results, that I was open to whatever the universe might send; I just wanted to say it out loud, to all of them, so they would be witnesses to my sending of a clear message.

One month later I asked my friend Michelle if she knew where I could meet available guys. She suggested online dating. I signed up on two websites. Within four days James e-mailed me.

Within the first month of dating it was clear to both of us that we were meant to be together, one day at a time.

Everything I asked for came true in our relationship, and I was grateful. And I always remembered that it was not a set of rules or a book or a list that got me there; rather, it was the desire to be true to myself, a willingness to be open, and an open-minded attitude to let a third party in: let a higher power play into our love and offer our love to it.

At the one-month mark, I told James that I wanted to do a ceremony to express gratitude for the love we felt for each other and the miraculous things that seemed to confirm to us every day that we were on the right track.

We made our own circle, just like the circle I had made earlier with the group of people who supported me through my addiction.

James dressed in a jacket and dry-cleaned pants. I thought that was cute—he was taking it seriously. I liked that. I wore a long black dress and put on the nicest piece of jewelry I owned.

We made a big circle with candles in the living room and then, together, we entered and sat at the center.

We spoke in turns. I went first. I said I was grateful that we had been brought together and asked that we both help each other come closer to our own spirits and that, as a couple, we be used for the good of all. James reiterated the message, with fewer words. Then we kissed and had dinner. He cooked.

Five years later, we are still happily married.

What was my big secret?

When the groundwork is done, when we ask for help, when we surround ourselves with those who will respect our time to speak up and hear what we need to share, we are let in on a huge and powerful secret: we reach God much more easily through other people's ears.

You may want to read that again. And please don't just believe me—try it for yourself and see.

In the vulnerability of asking for what we want in front of others, with an open heart and humility, we bring the presence of our and their higher forms of energy into the space.

We create a space between two people (or more) so that a higher power can enter. In its presence, prayers are louder, stronger, and more effective.

With the right intent, with the right inner No—in this case, no to addiction—the Yes you've always been looking for happens.

TESTING THE BIG SECRET
FOR YOURSELF

CLAUDIA: If there is something you want to attract in your life, instead of taking my word for it, try it.

In reading this book, you have probably already begun to think of those people who are supportive of you and will listen to you. Maybe you even have a support group. If you don't, work at creating one or at nurturing a friendship, because this is at the root of it all. Even though finding out what we need or want comes from silence, manifestation never works in solitude. We need other people.

Once you have one friend or a group of people with whom you feel safe, try it. Tell the people in front of you that you would like to ask God for something, and that even though it may sound strange, you want them to bear witness to your clear desire to manifest something in your life. Tell them you have chosen them because you know you can trust them.

Then say it out loud: "I am ready for this (say what you want). I want to manifest it in my life, and my friend is a witness that I am inviting this energy in. Thank you."

Thank your friend(s) or support group for participating in your ritual. Let it go. Be present. Witness the circumstances of your life as they develop over the next few weeks. Open yourself to life and see what happens.

Surrender to the words you said. They are out there now, bringing opportunities to you. Say yes to those opportunities because now you are ready.

Saying No at the
First Sign of Danger

CLAUDIA: When I signed up for online dating, I began meeting many men. I met them just for one hour, and for one cup of tea. There were no strings attached, and of course it was always in a public place. I figured one hour would be enough time to see if there was chemistry or not, and if there wasn't, there would be no long commitment of time or money for either party. It seemed like a fair arrangement. And it worked well.

More important, I knew that when a man told me who he was in this very first and short encounter, I would believe him.

In fact, one time I didn't even need an hour.

That was the case with Jake. Jake and I had agreed to meet on a Saturday at 5 P.M. at a coffee shop in Hoboken. As I was getting ready to drive to the coffee shop, I received an e-mail from him that said, "Sorry, I think I changed my mind about meeting you. Take care, wish you all the best. JK."

I called him at once because I was confused. He told me that the letters at the end of the sentence (JK) had meant "just kidding." His name being Jake, I had assumed they were his initials.

As I understood it, 15 minutes before our first date, he was indeed probably "just kidding." The thing was, the joke was on me. We weren't laughing together, and that did not feel good. My gut had already spoken. And when the gut says something, we all better pay close attention. This was a No. Being sober and without the desire to control anything allowed me to tell Jake, in a calm way, that I knew it would not work out.

Cutting losses early, given the evidence, would be beneficial not just for me but also for him. It would free us both to continue on the road to what we wanted, which was not the same thing.

He said that he was already driving, and he would have to turn around and drive all the way back for lots and lots of miles. For about a fraction of a second, I felt a tingle of guilt, but then I remembered from his profile that he lived no more than a few miles away from the coffee shop.

At his play on guilt, my gut pulled me again. But I was cool, and I didn't need to try to change him or make him understand anything. I told him I understood that he was already driving but that this was my decision. And by the way, I would have said no to a date under those circumstances even if it were a much longer drive. Distance makes no difference when we know, in our gut, that something is a No.

In disbelief, he insisted, as if some rule or technique he had followed to put me down was not working as he had anticipated. He seemed puzzled. I told him that my intuition said no.

He asked, "Hasn't your intuition ever been wrong?"

"I can't believe you are actually giving me the chance to answer that question," I said.

There was a silence. He did not hang up. He wanted to know. He was still listening. Wow!

And so I answered: "It's only when I haven't followed my intuition, Jake, that things have gone completely wrong. It's when I force things to go the way I want them to go, ignoring that pull in my stomach that senses something funny, that I mess up. It's when I follow the wrong kind of thinking—Oh, I will let this one slide even though it bothers me—that I end up starved and crying. I've done this many times; I will not do it again. Thank you, but no thank you. Good-bye."

When someone tells you who he is, the way Jake had just told me unmistakably, believe him. Don't blame him, and don't criticize him; he is also learning. Just let him go. He will figure it out.

Oh, and let's get clear on something. Women will also tell you who they are in this way. Actions, words, being on time or not, playing games or not, all of these details reveal us.

People who are disrespectful or manipulative early on are likely to continue the pattern. Take them at face value.

---- **EXERCISE** ----
SAY IT OUT LOUD

JAMES: Whenever I feel abused or disrespected, I go into a cycle of thinking that is difficult to stop. If only I had said this, or if only I had showed up later, or if only . . .

Some thoughts get stuck in our heads. Like a piece of paper stapled to a phone pole advertising a bad rock concert.

When you next think about the person (or the thought), whisper in your head, "No."

If you think again about the person, whisper in your head somewhat louder, "No."

And then louder.

And then actually whisper it aloud.

Then louder.

Then louder.

You will eventually stop thinking about that person.

For now.

Saying No to Jealousy

JAMES: Sometimes I am randomly jealous of people who have inherited a billion dollars. And then I get ashamed of feeling so jealous. *I'm better than that,* I mistakenly think.

Sometimes I am jealous of people who look better than me. *People who look great can have the entire world,* I think. *Why can't I have the entire world?*

Sometimes I am jealous of the many people who do things I wish I had done but didn't and now regret not doing. *Why those people? Why not me?!*

I try to be perfect. I try to grab the imperfections before anyone sees them and put them in my pocket. Hide them.

I should never *be jealous,* I think. But then my pocket overflows, and I'm a mess. I can't deny it.

Jealousy and anger and envy are road maps to your insides. It's never about the other people. I don't even know the other people. They have their own problems. Or not. Not my business!

Jealousy is the road map to the place where I feel unloved. Maybe I feel like I can't be loved unless I have billions. Or I look like a movie star. Or I have 20 best-selling books.

I can't fool myself. I can't say, "I shouldn't be envious of that." Because my body will say, "Tough! I am envious of that!" Your body knows when you are lying to it.

A therapist once told me, "The roots of this might go way back. Might go back to your toddler years."

That seems like a lot of work to me. And a lot of therapy. Like maybe I wasn't breast-fed enough and we'll figure that out—two years from now, one day a week, at hundreds of dollars a session. Who knows? The roots of envy can be anything. But I have to go to work today. The one thing I can choose is not to be ashamed of it. To say, "Okay, this is my challenge for the day." To accept it.

I have a problem with my relationship toward money. Thank you, jealousy, for pointing it out to me. It's true.

I have a problem about my looks. Ever since some girl ran out screaming from art camp when I told her I liked her and she said, "Not in a million years!" Thank you, jealousy. Apparently my looks were still good enough to help me meet a good woman. Maybe it's my sense of humor.

The jealousy is unavoidable. So take it for what it is: a road map to get yourself out of prison. Here's how to approach it:

a) Jealousy is a guide to what is going on inside of you.

b) It's never about the other person.

c) Never gossip about the people you feel jealous of. They don't care about what you think. And what they think about you is none of your business.

d) Everyone feels jealousy. We're human. Join the club.

e) Every con has a pro. Ask: what is good about your jealousy? If I don't have enough, maybe it means I can redefine "enough."

There's a story about Joseph Heller, the author of *Catch-22*, finding himself at a party made up of a bunch of Wall Street hedge-fund managers. A man comes up to him and points to a young guy in his 20s. The man says, "See that guy over there? He made more money last year than you will make in a lifetime of writing your books."

Heller turns to the man and says, "I have one thing that he will never have."

The man laughs and says, "What?"

Heller says, "Enough."

You can't get rid of the jealousy. This is another emotion that is not an on-off switch; it's a dimmer switch. You can dim the jealousy by exercising your abundance muscle.

ENOUGH!

JAMES: Go ahead: take a deep breath.

Find the areas in your life where you have "enough" (or more than enough). List them. This is where you are abundant.

Find the areas where you need to define your "enough." List them. These are the areas where you could be abundant, but you may not have clearly defined what abundance means to you. Maybe you don't need a hundred friends. Or a billion dollars. Or a screenplay produced by Hollywood.

Often, the less you need, the more abundance you have.

Saying No to Self-Sabotage

CLAUDIA: Kamal is a highly successful entrepreneur. A while back when things were going extremely well with his business, he met a woman he was convinced was the one for him.

He pursued her. She seemed to respond well at first, but then she withdrew and stopped returning his calls. Eventually she started dating other men.

One afternoon, Kamal and I met by the ocean. He had just gotten a text message from her; she said she didn't want to see him again. It was not the first text message of that kind. He was on the brink of tears.

"Think of your life as a train station," I said. "You are on the platform and you see a train approaching. You really want this train to be your train. You like the way it shines and how it seems so cool and strong—you are convinced it is the one that will take you home. And so you start making signals to it, and then you even start jumping up and down close to the tracks.

"But this train is not meant to stop here. The conductor of the train is confused. She starts to slow down and wonders what you are doing. She is nervous.

"Sensing that the train is not stopping, you jump onto the tracks, to the horror of all the people around you, and make even bigger arm signals while you jump up and down. By now the horrified conductor is calling the police and pressing all sorts of red buttons. Emergency vehicles are arriving on the scene. Everything is coming to a halt.

"Meanwhile, the train that is meant for you, the one that is your train by divine design, is right behind this one. Only you cannot see this because you are too busy causing unnecessary drama.

"Your train is waiting somewhere, feeling lonely, unable to pull into your station. The conductor of the train that is meant for you wonders what may be causing the delays. She longs to arrive home, and all the while it is *you* who is causing the traffic jam, because you just can't stop jumping up and down."

To say no to self-sabotage, get out of the train tracks and accept the flow of life. Let the train continue, wish it well as it leaves, and trust that yours is coming. That's all it takes.

Fear of No

JAMES: Often we are afraid to be told no. If we ask someone on a date, they might say no. When we go for a job interview, they could reject us. When we paint our masterpiece, the world might hate it.

And don't think that people don't know this. There are entire areas of psychology taught in schools, books, at seminars (sales seminars, negotiating seminars, *dating* seminars, and so on) about how to take advantage of people's fear of hearing the word *no*.

Our minds and bodies are taught to please more than they are taught to take chances. We are taught to stay in our uniform of sameness.

But if everyone is the same at a party, how will you know if there is a special unique someone there who matches your own special uniqueness?

The No of sex, the No of creativity, the No of abundance, is about finding out who you are so you can take off the uniform and not be afraid.

Why include sex on this list? Because sex is a place where our conditioning to please can be especially strong.

But if all you do is please the other at the expense of express-ing what you want—which flows from who you are—then even-tually you won't be happy. Sex (like any interaction between any two people) is intimate, and your partner will pick up on your unhappiness but might not be able to do anything about it. He or she can't read your mind.

Eventually you are left with two unhappy people.

And eventually two unhappy people will do things they think will make them happy. They might lie to each other to get what they want elsewhere. They might do things that will ultimately make them unhappy, all because they were afraid of hearing "No."

Sex is our rawest, most primal energy. It's how we got here. And how our parents got here. And their parents. All the way back to . . . who knows? The missing link!

But sex is just one frequency. Then there's creativity. Then there's laughter. Then there's money. Then there's the value you deliver to those around you. Then there's your contribution to society.

When you add your own unique value to society, you will get rewarded for it. That reward might be in the form of money, or it might not. But value begets value. People need to pay the bills. Being able to stand up, stand out, and say no to conformity simply helps pay the bills.

But first is getting over the fear.

The metaphor of sex applies to all of your interactions. If you are afraid of your touch being rejected for long enough, your touch turns into sandpaper. Say no to the fear of "No."

It's not that all life should be fun. It's that all life should be fearless.

— EXERCISE —
DARING TO TRY NEW IDEAS

Try this today.

Write down ten ideas for your job (or for someone else's job) that you think will add above-and-beyond value.

Write down the ten next steps for those ideas.

Write down the ten people you need to share these ideas with.

Write to those people.

Don't be afraid.

The worst they can do is say no.

— THIRD —

THE NO TO PHONY STORYTELLING

*You have the right to ask for
what you want and choose which
stories you believe in . . .*

JAMES: I was sure I would never date a woman who spoke English as a second language. She would be too hard to understand. I'd have to keep repeating myself. I'd have to keep saying, "What?" Imagine being married and always saying, "What?"

After my first date with Claudia, I was talking to a friend of mine and I told him Spanish was Claudia's first language. He said, "I guess that one is over."

Now I'm married to Claudia. I like her accent.

I am wrong almost all of the time.

Every five years all the science textbooks in school have to be thrown out. Science is constantly wrong or having to be updated.

In 1980 many thought a personal computer would be useless.

Newton was replaced by Einstein was replaced by quantum mechanics was replaced by . . .

Everyone thought the economy would disappear in 2009.

Sometimes Western medicine is right. Sometimes Eastern medicine is right.

In the 1970s people wrote books saying the world would have no food by 1980. Or that the world would be overpopulated.

Most people think marriage will last forever.

Most people think their children can do no wrong.

Family thinks you should show up at every wedding and for every family occasion.

Everyone is wrong almost all of the time and it makes zero sense to argue with them. They are happy being wrong. It fulfills needs they have.

My parents wanted me to get good grades, go to graduate school, get a good job, get married, own a home, rise up at my job, have kids, and live near them. They tried to dictate my entire life before I was even born. Their life wasn't happy. But maybe they could *force* mine in some way. Direct it. Control it.

How often are our choices planned by people who are themselves unhappy, sick, worried about their debts, unhappy in their marriages, or unhappy in their jobs? Should we let these people tell us what should we do with our lives? Impose their stories on us? Are they right about us even though they are wrong about themselves?

I don't want to waste my time getting angry or arguing with people. Or trying to convince people they are wrong about their plans for me. None of that is fun. I just choose not to listen to them. It's a big world. When one door shuts, ten more doors open. When one person hates me because I won't do what he or she thinks is right, I have another seven billion people I can choose from to pick as people I want to be around.

People (including me in the past) instinctively follow what has been imposed on them by institutions, parents, colleagues, schools, culture, false anger and dreams, and on and on. But each of us is unique, and we have our own path, regardless of the paths of others. You have to find your uniqueness.

I want to do what makes me feel at peace. Even if it means sometimes saying no to everyone I love. To all of the stories they tell.

Because that's proof that I love myself.

— EXERCISE —
OPINIONS

The next time someone has an opinion you strongly disagree with, try this:

- Don't argue; it's pointless. You will *never* change their mind.

- Let them state their opinion. Try to learn one thing from it. Try to respect one angle of their point of view.

- Everyone just wants to be heard.

- Listen.

The Assertive No

JAMES: Let's set aside the selfishness argument for now. We will address that. What follows are some "rules." You don't have to follow them. We're all free people.

Rule #1: Don't do anything you don't want to do.

When you agree to do something you don't want to do, you will resent the person who asked you to do it. You will grow to hate the activity. It will drip like a burning candle into your heart until you are burning with hate for yourself. Your simple act of what you thought was kindness, a simple Yes, will set you on fire.

Not only that, but other people will stop trusting you.

Don't do it.

But what if you have to?

For instance, many people don't want to go to school.

Okay, don't. Don't go.

Let the other 20 million kids go to school and learn to wear the uniform of society. You can do something different. Have an adventure, stand out, create something, and make yourself into a story.

One person gets to fly through space. The rest of the planet looks up from the earth and wonders what it would be like to do that.

"But I can't do that!" Okay, I believe you. Maybe it's because of your family. We know about family.

Stop anyone in the street and ask, "How well do you get along with your family?"

At first they will say, "Fine!" because they will be thinking, *Who is this strange person who just stopped me in the street and asked me about my family?* And it's almost a crime to not love and respect your family.

But I don't know anyone who can say "My family is perfect." Even blood bonds often break down somewhere along the way.

Our families are usually the greatest challenge we were sent to earth to solve. Face it. Family is tough. We spend a lot of time with our brothers and sisters and parents and cousins and uncles and so on.

Inevitably, jealousies and conflicts come up. Inevitably, she has this and he doesn't. Or she wanted this but he got it. Or he ignored me when I needed him, or she tried to stop me when I needed to . . . and so on.

So our families are where we first get to practice our No. Our assertive No. Our No to other people's stories.

The bonds of family become much stronger if you learn how to say no to them and how to forge new familial and familiar relationships with the people you love, the people you grew up with. Then people learn to trust you.

But family (and later your friends, or your colleagues, or your bosses, or your schools, and so on) will try anything and everything to dull your No first. They do this because they think they are protecting you or themselves. But often they are doing it because they are unconscious. Don't blame them.

They will threaten to kill themselves unless . . .

They will threaten to kill you unless . . .

They will cry, they will manipulate, and they will destroy.

When we are young and can't protect ourselves, some of our families are more violent than others. And when we are bursting through the egg and coming to life and beginning to fly from the nest, it's not physical violence but emotional violence that fights our No.

And if even that doesn't work, there's mental violence: you have to do this because X! And X is usually a well-thought-out reason—a very solid reason. You must do X because X is how it's done.

And finally, if that doesn't work, then spiritual violence will fight the No—the imperative to honor thy family.

Although in every religion there is evidence to the contrary. In the most sacred text in Hinduism, the *Bhagavad Gita*, Arjuna gives up in the middle of battle rather than fight his cousins, his grandfather, and all his relatives. Then his humble chari-oteer, named Krishna, turns into Vishnu/God and explains to him why this has to happen. Why it is his mission to fight on the battlefield.

He is not saying "Kill your family." Nobody would say that. He is saying that to reach your own divinity, you have to learn to say no and stand up for what is right for you in this moment. You need to learn who you are. And for Arjuna, at this time, it means fighting the battle.

In Buddhism, the young Siddhartha has to leave his beautiful wife, his loving father, his newborn son, and all of his possessions in order to achieve the immortality he finds six years later while sitting in silence. This doesn't mean you need to leave your fam-ily to find enlightenment—far from it. But symbolically, nobody can deliver wisdom to you except you. The being who finds peace inside himself needs nobody to tell him what to do, nobody to project their own fantasies onto him.

In Judaism, there is Abraham leaving the idolatry of his father to strike out on his own. There is Isaac versus Isaiah. There is Jacob versus Esau. There are the sons of Jacob versus Joseph. There are the sons of David versus each other. And so on.

In Christianity, there is the wedding Jesus attends. His mother and brothers are outside and want to see him. Jesus lets them wait and turns to his apostles and says, "You are my family now." We go through life creating new families, learning from them, and moving on.

But every religion actually started with a No first: to family and then to establishment. And then to friends. And then to culture.

This is not to say join a religion. In fact, religion often becomes the establishment within a few short generations after its creator leaves.

As you reach inside to find the No, you will often find yourself at odds with establishment. Be prepared.

That's right; we only had one rule in mind when we said here are some rules.

So Rule #2: Don't forget Rule #1.

---- EXERCISE ----

WHAT DOES SOCIETY WANT
YOU TO SAY YES TO?

First of all, take a big deep breath because while this exercise may sound simple, it involves going to the root of your beliefs, which can be unsettling. So choose the time and space for it carefully.

Do this with a small pad to write on. Ideally a waiter's pad.

Make a list of the things society tells you to do:

- Get a job

- Buy a home

- Have children

- Get married

- Get an education

- Vote

- Fight the bad guys in a war

- Respect the government

And so on. Come up with others. Come up with as many as possible.

None of these things is bad. Some of them might be quite important and good for you.

Take some time to reflect on them. One at a time. Think about how you feel about these things. Is a college education necessary for your children, for instance? Do you need to own a home to be happy? Consider both sides of the story.

(continued on following page)

Going through this exercise is revolutionary because it will bring you face to face with what *you* believe in. Independently of what you've been told. It might open your eyes over the course of weeks or months to points of view you did not even know you had. You may come across articles or books that show other ideas; you may (watch out) even realize you no longer agree with things you previously did!

There is a psychological law that says we all tend to follow our own ways of thinking without changing because we want to appear "consistent." But consistency can sometimes represent a burden that might drag us to dark places.

At first, realizing that the things we strongly believe in can also be seen as "stories" can be shocking. Don't worry if you find yourself unsettled or perhaps even angry, if you finally get a glimpse into the fact that, for example, money is only a story that has been going around for no more than a couple thousand years. There was no money before then.

When we begin to question things to their very core, we can be left a little disoriented. This is good because suddenly a new freedom is appearing. Even though we will still continue to love our children, vote, or buy a home, we can at least know that we have explored the issue and become very clear on how we feel about it.

Doing this exercise with a commitment to truth and revealing our own values may mean we have to take responsibility for them, and maybe make changes in order to be true to ourselves.

Becoming true to ourselves frees us because it gives us the opportunity to find our own power in our individuation. It lets us know that we are allowed to have our own creative and thinking process and still be functioning members of the society we choose to live in.

When we actually look at what we believe as opposed to what we've been told to believe, we realize there is a lot more to us than made-up stories. When we choose to accept the ideas that really resonate with us, we are acting from our inner Yes and from freedom.

Saying No to Being a Slave

JAMES: The average person works at a job. Fine, you might say, a job is a lot different from slavery: I can take a water break, for instance. And sometimes go to the bathroom. And when I talk to people who are the same sex as me, there aren't even any rules governing what I can say. And I get a salary. Great.

If, like most Americans, you have a mortgage, there goes at least 20 percent of your salary, sometimes more. Your company likes you to own your house because you are less likely to quit.

Then there are student loans you are paying off. For the first time ever, more than half of the unemployed have college degrees. That is pretty scary. You got this degree because (in part) you thought it would get you a job. But it didn't guarantee anything, and now you have to pay for it. Some percentage of your salary is sliced off every month to pay for that degree.

Then some portion of your salary goes toward health, upkeep of your relationships (they always cost money; this is not being cynical, just realistic), and your transportation to your job (they force you to pay your own way to your slave quarters).

How much goes to you? You wake up before dawn. You travel. You work hard. You come home late. You're feeling stuck. You're mildly depressed and may take medication for this. And you have trouble sleeping and digesting.

Shouldn't you get paid more?

Then there's behavior. "I can do whatever I want," I used to say. In fact, when I was at a job I felt free. I could "sneak out" at 4 P.M. I could take lots of breaks. Vacations were big.

But did you look at the manual? There's a big manual. And sometimes there are workshops devoted to going over the manual.

For example, they have rules about how you may or may not talk to people; everything is regulated.

You can't talk to your boss a certain way. Because for all of your slaving away, all he has to say is "You're fired" and that's the end.

You can't wear what you want. Most office situations have a uniform, either explicit or implicit.

You can't be friends with whom you want. You're mostly just friends with the people you spend your day with—the other slaves. When they leave the job you never talk to them again.

You can't be creative when inspiration hits. "Anything done on equipment owned by the company is intellectual property owned by the company." Good luck arguing about that one.

You can't have an office romance even though those are the only people of the opposite sex you know. For one thing you might get fired. And Human Resources can read all of your e-mails.

If you want more money, you have to beg for it. There are entire seminars created just to teach people how to ask for 5 percent more money at work. People are scared to death to ask.

And by the time you get home to have real social interactions, you're tired and bitter and angry about work.

Isn't there another way?

Yes. There are *always* alternatives.

Now, more than ever, most people can make more money by being creative and figuring out how to offer services on their own.

Money won't solve all of your problems, but it will solve your money problems. Don't let them take your money so they can keep you in slavery.

You want to own your time. To own your work. To own the value you create for others. To own your thoughts. To protect yourself so nobody can fire you. Not to be owned by the bank or the government or a boss. Not to be owned by your relationships.

"I can't just quit my job!" you might say.

And we agree with this. Don't quit.

But . . .

Start by being an explorer.

We live in a $51 trillion economy. You helped create it, just as slaves and death and misery helped create the beautiful pyramids. But 90 percent of what you create is taken from you.

Start to explore what parts you can take back. Work every day on ideas. List every interest you've had since you were a kid.

If you are having trouble with this, go to a bookstore. Look at every book that interests you and write it down. List every business or job that can be started from that interest. Read every day about your interests. And if you are still having trouble with your interests, focus on your health instead. List all the things you can do to make yourself healthier.

If you get bored with what you are reading, then no problem, find another interest to read about.

Don't be angry at the people at work, even your boss. They are all slaves also. You need to break free from them. Don't waste your free thoughts on the other slaves with their Rolex shackles.

Study the lives of people who aren't slaves. What did they do? Study the people who seem to have broken free. What are they doing? Keep working on your idea muscle. You do this by writing down ten ideas a day. It doesn't matter what the ideas are. It doesn't matter if they are good or bad. This is just exercising. This is physical therapy applied to the mind so that your idea muscle doesn't atrophy.

I did this myself. I worked my mental muscle every single day, hard. And in six months my life changed completely. In fact, as I've said, *every* six months my life changes completely.

Sixteen years ago my boss yelled at me. He's a good guy and has since broken free himself, but one time he yelled at me and I couldn't yell back or I would risk being fired. I felt like crying. Actually, I did cry.

So I went to the library on Forty-First Street and Fifth Avenue. I found a science fiction book I had read once as a kid. It had that cellophane wrapping and a library card in it. And it had that smell you get when you open the aging yellow pages.

I went three or four levels down, to my private bathroom in the library, my sanctum sanctorum. And I sat there and I read about a man who lived forever and was happy. And the world disappeared and for a brief moment I was no longer a slave.

From that moment on, I plotted my escape. And every day since, I figure out new ways to escape, new ways to be free. New ways to own my world.

THE DAILY PRACTICE TO GET UNSTUCK

This is what worked for us to get healthy. To take a step back and realize how to get through the obstacles in our lives. Then to push forward and become idea machines, able to execute these ideas with health and security, and finally able to surrender to a universe whose best intentions align with our own.

Make sure you check the box on these items every day . . .

. . . *Especially* if you want to escape the 9-to-5 world:

- Physical: Sleep well, exercise when you can, eat well, and avoid addictions.

- Emotional: Only associate and engage with the people you love, the people who inspire you, and the people you inspire.

- Mental: Always be reading; always be writing down new ideas. Ten ideas a day.

   This is critical. You need to bring your idea muscle into great shape. If coming up with ten ideas sounds too hard, then come up with twenty. You need to practice this to the point where ideas will be pouring out of you like mangos in tropical countries falling onto the street, free for everyone to admire and taste their sweetness.

   That is how you become the idea *magnet,* the person everyone wants to hang out with, the person who can create new things, the person who can create a new and useful businesses that in turn can bring you money so you can quit your job.

(continued on following page)

- Spiritual: We will cover this in much more detail in a later chapter, but for now, cultivate a sense of gratitude for the abundance you have right now. Surrender to what you can't control.

What if you are in a crisis? It's too hard to do this!

The trick is to catch your thoughts as they happen. Even the thoughts of pain. You will always have painful thoughts and experiences.

But slow down. Take a deep breath. And surrender.

Just run through the checklist: Are you doing the Daily Practice today? If not, no pressure. Try to fit it back in. Just do one item on the above list. Or two. Eventually you will be back in shape.

Pain, emotional or mental pain (worry, anxiety, regret) in particular, is an example of the brain trying to protect you. Poor brain! It is only trying its hardest.

It thinks that by bringing up painful thoughts it will keep you from touching the fire again.

We love our brains, but sometimes they are annoying.

So you have to domesticate your brain the way you domesticate a dog.

USEFUL/NOT USEFUL

An alternative here is the useful/not useful technique. This will turn you into a powerful "brain whisperer."

With each thought that comes up, label it either useful or not useful.

If I worry about two people talking behind my back, this is not useful. It's none of my business what they think of me. I don't want to be curious about the negative opinions other people have of me. Or else I'd be curious all my life about all the wrong things.

If I wake up in the middle of the night worried about a deal or a relationship this is not useful, I make an appointment with myself to deal with the issue at 3 P.M. instead of 3 A.M. Often by 3 P.M. I am thinking of something else.

If I worry about how much money I will have five years from now, this is not useful. If I worry about what I did at the party last night, this is not useful.

What is useful then? Functional things. If I say, "I need to pack lunch for the kids right now," that is useful. Unless I can teach them to pack lunch for themselves, which will be useful at some point as well.

What is actually going on here is that you are separating yourself from your brain.

Just as you can control your breath when you need to, it's important to be able to control your brain when you need to.

Often the brain doesn't need this. Just as you often don't need to tell your breath what to do. But sometimes you need to get involved.

Most people don't do this. Most people go through their days with the brain completely in charge. You can see them in the street,

(continued on following page)

their eyes glazed as they wend their way through regrets of the past and anxieties of the future. They don't know how to escape.

Saying no to others means first saying no to your brain—to the anxieties and the regrets and the not-useful thoughts. Practicing exercises like this one will help you do that.

Then you will be able to climb above ground. You will see the beautiful and enormous world that is there waiting for you. You are on the path of No, and yes, to be corny about it—there is no return.

Three No's and One Yes

JAMES: Here's a problem I have: I agree to things. Lots of things. Meet me for coffee? Okay. Be an advisor for my company—it will only take one hour a week? Okay. Speak at my conference? Okay. Babysit my kids? Never in a million years (okay, I don't agree to absolutely everything).

Do you have a tendency to say yes to too many things? Do you find it hard to say no? Do you think you will be rude or that others won't like you?

If so, try this. You are entitled to three No's for every one Yes in your life.

This worked when I brought on clients with my initial business. It has worked when I have sold businesses. It has worked when I have met or invested in new people. It has worked in my relationships. Three No's and then one Yes.

It's not a trick. It's not designed to make the people who are asking you desperate. Let's break it down:

1. You have to say the first No because you don't have enough information. I simply never know enough about the people or the companies involved or the woman I'm dating or the friend I'm meeting for the first time to say yes.

Sometimes you get very excited, but the reality is that you never know enough in that first meeting. Even if you are selling yourself, as is the case when you are pitching a new client, you have to say no the first time or "I need to discuss this with my partners" or "This is all good, but let me think about the best way I can help you because I want to be fair."

Prepare your words in advance. "I have to say no right now until I consult with my partner/friend/husband/parent."

2. The second No occurs because now you know the person but you don't know all the details. You are still learning the terms of the relationship and how things will work. You might be in business together for a long time. It doesn't matter if you are applying for a janitor position or to be CEO of a company; you need to know the details.

3. The third No occurs because you simply have to decide: "Do I like this person I'm about to say yes to?" Otherwise, you may get involved in dealings with someone you don't like. Here's where you can say, "Give me a little time." Time is not a hard thing for people to give. I can't even hold time between two of my fingers. That's how small it is.

As the expression goes, life is too short. I don't like to work with people I don't like.

Well, you may say, not everyone has that choice.

My response: Okay. You might not have that choice, but I do. And it's only because I started following my own advice, doing the Daily Practice to stay healthy, and manifesting my own choices.

In fact, the only times in my life when:

- I lost all my money

- I became desperate for opportunity

- I lost friends, relationships, family

were the times when I said yes too much and too quickly.

I would give up my personal power. Not that the goal is to have power over people—that is the wrong way to use the Power of No.

The goal is to reclaim power for yourself. To take a step back and ask deep down, "What do I want?" To say no, not to push people away and make them desperate, but to let them know that relationships are important to you. That your relationship with them is important to you and requires respect from you.

The benefit is that if they walk away after the first No, or the second No, or even the third No, then there was never a Yes that would have worked for you in the long run. If you say yes when you don't want to, you will quickly learn to hate everyone around you, including the person you see when you look in the mirror.

——— EXERCISE ———
BURN THE EXCUSES

Many people say, "But I can't change!"

I'm too old, or I have too many responsibilities, or I don't have enough education. Or people will laugh at me.

Excuses are leaks in a boat. When you cover one, another pops up, and it's even bigger. It's hard to keep the boat repaired and get safely to shore if you have an excuse mind-set.

Here is a suggestion:

- Choose a time and space for reflection.

- Light a candle and set the mood.

- Invite your spirit in. Say a little prayer.

- Get a piece of paper and an envelope.

- Write down all of your excuses for why you can't change your life. Go ahead. It will be fun.

- Put the paper with the excuses into the envelope. This is a sacred envelope now. It has all of your excuses.

- Close your eyes and take a deep breath. Feel the envelope in your hand.

- Say, "Excuses, I have to send you away now. We've been through a lot together, but now we must part paths."

- Take the envelope and throw it in the garbage. Take the garbage out of your house.

- Blow out the candle. This is you symbolically burning your excuses.

Whenever one of those excuses comes up again, realize that it is no longer yours to claim.

The light from that candle has now replaced the excuses. If they still keep popping up in your head, hold out your hand. Say, "Let there be light," and picture the excuses burning up.

It's not corny because it works.

Note that this is a practice. Your excuses may burn up the first day or they may not. That's okay. Practice doesn't make perfect. But practice will make permanent. Bit by bit.

Complaining Is a No!

CLAUDIA: I attended a workshop once in which the facilitator gave all of us a rubber band to wear on our wrists. For the duration of the week, whenever we found ourselves complaining, we were to stretch the rubber band far and wide and let it go, so it would hit us.

It was a slap on the wrist, and an excellent way to teach me, at the body level, that complaining hurts. It was saying a firm No to all complaints.

Complaining sucks the air out of any new possibilities that may appear in the present moment; it drags things down into a depressive mode and leaves us drained.

Complaining is reacting to the pain we are already feeling, and in a negative way. It is a sure way to double the pain rather than doing what works, which is this: observe and release.

When we stop the complaining, we begin to see every situation as an opportunity. We shift our perception and we experience the miracle of a different way of seeing things instead of the old tired ways, which we know never work.

When we stop complaining, we align ourselves with absolute intelligence. We open the door to new ideas rather than shutting them down.

Of course this does not mean we let everyone walk all over us. Complaining is different from standing up for ourselves. If someone is trying to steal our energy, then of course we speak up and do what we can to stop that.

Complaining, however, is a low-frequency energy, and one that never works for anything.

When we stop complaining we are trusting that there is a better way and we are ready to hear it.

── EXERCISE ──
THE NO COMPLAINTS DIET

Complaining is draining.

Attempt one week of living without any complaints whatsoever. If you feel negative reactions arising, do your best to stop them. If they become full-blown complaints, then you have to start again, at hour zero.

Be careful of what you say in situations where small talk is expected. These are times when everybody is particularly vulnerable to casual complaining.

Talk about the weather if you have to say something. If the other person tries to steer you in a negative direction, change the conversation. If that does not work, tell the person that you are not comfortable talking negatively today because you are on a complaint diet. Say it. Be different. That will instantly shift the conversation.

Replace a complaint thought with one of gratitude or compassion. This is the true law of attraction.

When the week is up, take stock of how well you did.

Repeat for the rest of your life.

When to Say No to the Rules

JAMES: We grow up with rules, and we hate them.

Little kids need rules. For instance, don't cross the road without holding an adult's hand. Don't drink more than one cup of soda. Don't steal from the drugstore.

As we get older we realize that some rules have morphed into laws ("Don't kill anyone!") and with good reason. This is how society operates. We've all implicitly agreed that the way millions of humans will get along is by following a set of laws. This is how I know that complete strangers won't kill me (most of the time). The laws aren't foolproof (someone can pretty easily kill me if they truly want to), but they hopefully dissuade us from those actions and set guidelines for living in a complex society.

But some rules attempt to govern your behavior in a more personal way. There's even a book, *The Rules,* about how you should act when dating. As opposed to just being yourself, there are "rules" to follow if you want the girl or the guy to like you and love you.

What happens when she finds the real you is another story. By that time there might not be a real you anyway. The source of many problems in relationships is that everyone wears masks at first in order to be liked.

If we don't like ourselves to begin with, the masks we wear will be gross distortions of who we are.

Eventually the masks come off. Then problems start. And this is not just in romantic relationships but in work relationships, family relationships, relationships with the institutions around us, with our neighbors, and so on.

The thing about rules is that they aren't absolute. An extreme example of this occurs in Science. Capitalizing "Science" almost makes it seem like it's a deity, but in our society, it does play the role of a deity. We think it makes the laws of weather and the universe, we think it determines what forces are at play that can create either good luck or calamity, and so on.

And yet, the "laws" of Science tend to change every five to ten years, and new textbooks have to be written. Einstein almost completely rewrote Newton, yet a few short years after Einstein, Heisenberg's "uncertainty principle" threw into jeopardy the "laws" of relativity.

We are poor predictors of the future. Most people think, *If I get into this school* or *If I meet the right guy* or *If I get the house of my dreams* or *If I have children,* they can finally achieve happiness.

We go through life with some basic guidelines (the rules) on how to achieve these things—get good grades, be nice to your boss, save up for a house, don't paint outside the lines—and eventually we get some or all of the items that are perceived to bring about happiness. It's very black and white.

But between black and white there is a beautiful spectrum. Not of grays but of all the colors of the universe. A color is a frequency on the spectrum. We each are ringing with our own perfect frequency on this spectrum. Our mission as human beings is to vibrate with our own frequency and not someone else's.

To help others, we must first make sure we are constantly nourishing the soul. Two farmers lived side by side. One did the proper work in digging his well; the other did it more haphazardly. During a drought, the former who did the proper digging had enough water to survive. The other farmer had to go thirsty.

The Power of No is the power of discernment. With spiritual skepticism we develop the discernment to know which rules to say yes to, which rules to say no to, and which rules need to be completely rewritten to save the universe.

How to Know When to Break the Rules:

a) Use your assertive No. Never do anything you don't want to do. It's hard sometimes to say no to the things you don't want to do, so here are some guidelines:

  Sleep on it. Sleep regenerates every neuron in the brain devoted to creativity. Saying no often requires you to be creative.

  Be honest. Understand why you don't want to do something. Be able to express why.

  Delay. Delay doesn't mean "wait forever." It means "I need time to think about this." Use it wisely.

  Be loving. If people can't handle a No given with love, there were other problems in the relationship to begin with. What are those deeper problems?

  Surrender. You've said the No. Now wait for the results. Often the results will turn out to be better than you thought. Remember that we are poor predictors of the future. Both long and short term. We think the consequences might be bad if we say no. But actually we don't have a clue.

b) Do no harm. If an action you're considering carries the risk of harming someone, don't do it.

  And don't forget that the person you are most likely to harm is yourself. Make sure you don't do anything that can harm yourself.

  A simple example is crossing the street. If no cars are coming, then cross. Nobody is harmed. A more complicated example is when a competitor offers you a job but you are still employed and getting valuable information at the current job that could benefit the competitor. What rules are important to follow here? What disclosures are necessary?

We have no idea but using the guideline of "Do no harm" is a good road map.

c) Exercise compassion. You know the saying "They are just doing their job. Don't blame them." We don't know if you should blame them or not. But blaming won't help you find meaning in your life. It will only lead your brain down a path of self-destruction.

It's often hard to feel compassion for the people you despise most in life. But everyone is going through their own situation. Their own personal struggles with loneliness and isolation and fear. And then they die.

Don't feel pity toward your enemies, but don't waste time on blame either.

Practicing compassion toward the people around you, both good and bad, is a powerful technique. It doesn't make these people treat you any better. Who knows—they might treat you worse. But it does give you this amazing superpower very quickly: you can feel compassionate toward strangers who are trying to stand in your way.

Everywhere you go there are rules and there are gatekeepers of those rules: total strangers whose job it is to prevent you from doing something you want to do.

Showing compassion toward those gatekeepers will allow those gates to magically swing open more often than you can possibly hope to expect otherwise.

Why? Because the gatekeepers are not used to receiving a sudden onslaught of compassion or genuine love. Will they actually feel something different for you? Who knows? Who knows anything?

We only know what works in practice. We, the authors, break many rules. And we do it through the daily practice of cultivating compassion toward people who would not expect it.

"I thought compassion is supposed to be selfless. You make it sound selfish!?"

And our answer is: So what? Compassion is compassion. Does compassion have to be something that is not good for you? What if it turns out to be very good for you?

When something works, we use it.

This book is not about taking over the world, or saying no in an angry way to everyone around us. It is about taking care of ourselves. Which means not only respecting our current boundaries but also creating new ones, crazy ones, extra-dimensional ones.

Which means not falling into the camp of black or white, but finding our own special frequency, the one where we shine the brightest in this universe we have suddenly found ourselves in.

You find that frequency, where your inner No is, through the techniques we have described. Then you write the rules.

Because if you don't make your rules, someone else will.

Say No to Sudden Thought Attacks

JAMES: I wake up at three in the morning every day. I can't help it. As much as I focus on sleep hygiene, I almost have post-traumatic stress from the many, many times I've woken up in a panic at three in the morning.

Like the time I woke up when I was a day trader and went downstairs to see how the markets were doing. What the hell was I going to do at three in the morning?

What markets?

This was almost a decade ago. Well, it turned out there had been a terrorist attack in Turkey, so worldwide markets were falling. I called my business partner and woke him up at 3 A.M. so we could both be in a panic. We owned shares in all the markets and had to figure out how to sell.

Maybe the world was collapsing! What would we do?! We panicked and sold.

By 9 A.M., the terrorist attack, at least from a market perspective, was old news. Everything was coming back strong. I bought back, but I had wasted six hours worrying and panicking.

Another time, I was going broke. I woke up at three in the morning in a panic, as usual.

I added up all the money I had coming in. I added up money I had in the bank. I divided it by what I was spending each month,

I cut expenses and divided again. I mentally worked harder and added more. I subtracted and multiplied. I played with fractions.

But it was no good. I was going to go broke and then die.

I started to cry. Finally, I fell asleep right there on the table. There was simply nothing I could do.

When I woke up, there were pieces of paper all over the table with numbers on them. Numbers crossed off, numbers written down the edge. Asterisks next to some numbers. Parentheses around others. Some papers were crumpled on the floor.

But none of the papers meant anything.

And I don't mean this in a metaphorical way. I kept trying to find a single piece of paper that actually meant something. It was like going into the basement of that guy in the movie *A Beautiful Mind*. None of the papers were decipherable.

And, as usual, my worst fears didn't happen. They didn't even come close to happening.

These are 2 stories, but I have 50 of them. The time the IRS wrote me a letter and I decided that three in the morning was the best time to wake up and think about it. The time my girlfriend who was supposed to call me at 9 P.M. didn't call me and now it was 3 A.M. The time I had to go on TV the next day and I was scared. The time I was going through a divorce and was afraid I would never see my kids again.

Nothing ever happened that I predicted at three in the morning.

I'll say it again: Nothing I ever predicted at three in the morning ever came true.

Ever.

So here's what I do now, which you can use as an exercise.

I say to myself, "Nothing I ever predict at three in the morning comes true. I'm tired now and need to sleep.

"So I'm going to make an appointment with myself at three in the afternoon to focus on this burning issue."

— EXERCISE —
TAMING THE OVERTHINKING MIND

Being aware of the thoughts that flow through our minds is powerful because usually we just go through life as slaves to them.

Letting our thoughts go and being present without naming what is happening all the time gives us a rest and an opportunity to let something else in. Maybe wisdom, maybe peace.

It's estimated that the average person thinks as many as 70,000 thoughts a day.

- Practice ways you can edit that number down, the way a writer skillfully cuts down an overwritten novel.

- Notice whenever you are thinking many thoughts and when they are verging on panic.

- Take a deep breath, cut the thoughts down, and again practice shifting your perception to one of abundance and calm.

- Be aware that you are making a shift from panic (lots of thoughts) to abundance (fewer thoughts).

- Ask yourself, *What do I really need to understand?* And be quiet. Listen for the answers.

Saying No to Social Pressure

CLAUDIA: A few years ago the wife of an artist I admire very much invited me to a surprise dinner party to celebrate one of her husband's well-deserved awards.

At the time I was depressed, but I wanted to go for at least a few minutes to support my friend. When I arrived I didn't know anyone else there and felt awkward. Then I said hello to my friend and congratulated him. The party was on the late side for me, so I decided to leave early.

I could also feel my depression kicking in and knew that once the meal was served I would be trapped there for the night. I thanked his wife and mentioned I was going.

This is when all hell broke loose.

I don't remember the exact words she used, but anyone reading her face from afar could see she was telling me off. Raising her voice, she cut me with a sharp tongue and a high-handed tone: "You can't leave! The seating and food are all prepared."

Forty-plus years of living went out the window. I was not a woman, I was prey. I walked backward, inching toward the wall until my back was against the wood paneling and I had nowhere to go. "Okay," I said as something inside me crashed.

I could have just said no but I didn't know how. They didn't teach that at my school. When we were children we were taught to be polite, to be nice, and to say yes at all of the wrong moments. In that moment with my friend's wife, I was a child again.

I now know the key is to do what we call ABC: Acknowledge, Boundary, Close. Whenever you sense someone is about to start manipulating you, you need to go into ABC mode.

First the Acknowledge. I could've repeated what she said. Yes, a lot of work has gone into the situation (in this case, the dinner party), and it is wonderful.

Then the Boundary: "I have to leave in five minutes." The other person may or may not approve but that is no longer your problem. The benefits from doing this in your life will far outweigh the discomfort of that moment. Just keep repeating *ABC*.

Finally, the Close: After a few minutes, leave.

ABC is a very effective way of dealing with manipulative behavior. You first need to understand what is happening (recognize the onset of manipulation) because if you act immediately, without recognizing what you are feeling, without taking a breath, you are in danger of creating even more chaos.

Not being honest with yourself is how you say yes to everyone else but not to *you*. It's a form of self-harm.

If you don't say yes on your own terms, you are saying it on everyone else's terms, and the results will hurt you.

View these opportunities as education. View these obstacles as ways to learn how to grow. Without learning to say no, you can never learn to say a true Yes to *you*.

Saying No to Abusive People

How do you recognize an abusive person? These are some of the most common ways:

a) They try to make you feel guilty.

b) They try to make you angry.

c) They try to make you afraid.

d) They try to make you feel wrong.

e) They try to make themselves the victim.

f) They try to turn others against you.

g) In their possessed zombie bodies, they try to sound clever, and convincingly reasonable, to anyone who listens.

Always ask yourself: *How do I feel about myself when I am around this person? Do I feel good about myself?*

If the answer is no, you know you need to move away from the person. The key is not to engage. You need to quarantine the abusive person's disease and not let it spread. Otherwise it will make you sick, too.

You might try to feel compassion for these people. But that doesn't mean you need to spend time with them—or worse, save them.

Before we go further, let us just say that this is really hard. It's hard for us. It's hard for everybody.

It is especially hard because most of the time, these people are close family members, business partners, or the boss: someone we have to see every day. It is those who are closest to us, after all, who know where our buttons are.

Anger can also run through many generations. Evil has a way of feeding on new blood.

When an abusive person appears in your life, it doesn't matter who is at fault. That is *not* the point because it means you are engaging, discussing, and trying to be reasonable with an energy that knows nothing about reason.

Always say to yourself, *I'd rather be healthy than right.* Because the infection of someone so wounded will spread to you if you engage.

So, if you do have to deal with this person, use intermediaries as much as possible. If you need to communicate directly, keep it short and stick to the message.

This is a lot easier said than done, but then again, when one of these hard spiritual tasks comes to you, you can be sure that help is on the way if you ask for it. You are about to grow and become wiser.

An abusive person entering your life is a directive from Spirit pointing to errors you have made in the past, which brought you here, and giving you a chance to change course, learn, and look at things anew.

After you act from this new perspective, surrender the results.

This means don't get attached to any one outcome, for that is a sure way to be pulled back into trying to be "right" rather than healthy and happy.

What if this abusive person wants to come back into your circle, saying that he or she has changed?

Be careful. There is a cycle to the abusive relationship, one in which the abuser thinks he is now well, only to repeat the abuse once trust is restored. You could find yourself in the same situation you were in before. You can lose weeks, months, years of your life this way.

An abusive person's reappearance in your life may even require professional help, depending on the nature of the original abuse. You need to keep the boundaries extremely clear and monitor every step to see whether trust can be restored.

Often this is where you can use that second most important word. *Help.*

—◂ FOURTH ▸—

THE NO TO THE ANGERS OF THE PAST

You have the right to be honest, especially with yourself, and to respect your own timings, your rhythms, your nature . . .

Over the past three years James has answered tens of thousands of questions on our blogs, in seminars, online, and in talks.

The questions come in by the hundreds, from all over the world, and the topics range from relationships gone badly, to jobs people hate, to how to find a passion, to how to get out of the mess of being broke, lonely, and addicted.

All these questions together are like the pigments on a painting. When you step back a few feet and see the whole painting, you can see exactly where we are as a human race.

When you look carefully, it becomes very clear *where* we are hurting, *why* we are confused, and *what* is important to all of us, right now. We all want to heal. We all want to be the person we know, deep inside, we really are. We all want to shine. We all want to be loved. We all want to be proud of our impact on the world.

We are all trying hard, very hard. But many people feel they are stuck. They don't know how to move forward.

The fourth No meets us at our current level of evolution.

Even though all seven No's work together, and even though every one of us uses awareness from all of them at different times, there is a particular hierarchy to the No's.

The first level helps us with our open wounds and scars. We must patch those up to protect our very lives.

The second No redirects our energies from addictive or evasive temptations toward what is important to us, toward what we want to create.

The third No helps us become true individuals. We recognize that we don't need to be manipulated or pushed around. And now, as apprentices to the Power of No, we begin to learn how society has been manipulated by very deep forces that have spread from our most respected institutions into the deepest parts of our hearts.

Now our hearts are opening. Now we are learning not to resist the truth but to flow with it. This is where true abundance can be found.

Now is the time for us to reach a critical mass of awareness so we can transition from being *Homo sapiens* to becoming *Homo luminous*, shining our light on the world.

The Compassionate No

CLAUDIA: When my mother jumped to her death from the seventh floor of our apartment building, I was barely 18. I arrived at the scene two hours later.

She was still there, in the backyard of Apartment 1H, where her body had shattered a glass table. There was a police officer guarding the front door, blocking about 200 people who were drawn to the magnetism of a horrible event.

When I saw the officer blocking the door, I felt a rush of power, defiance, anger—an explosion of emotions. I was face to face with him in less than a second. I looked him in the eye and demanded to go in, to see for myself. I wanted to be in charge of my nightmare. Not him!

"You can't go in," he said, "because the police are investigating." His stance was firm, hands on his hips.

I went crazy. I told him that *that* was my mother, and I didn't care. I was going in, so help me God.

Then . . . the matrix melted.

His shoulders relaxed. He moved just a tiny bit out of the way and kept eye contact with me. Only this time, his eyes softened and a deep sadness came pouring out from him, straight into my heart. Then he whispered to me: "You don't want to see this."

I took two steps back, as if shot by an arrow. Still looking at him, I broke down because now it was real—and he was right: I didn't want to see it. I turned around to face my family and melted into tears.

It was the humanness in this officer that made me see that I was in shock. It was his ability to see eye to eye with me, broken heart to broken heart, that helped me take the right step, away from the apartment—not the fact that he was blocking the door. It was his honesty in trying to understand what I might have been going through—that was what touched me.

I think of him as an angel because he dropped all the demeanor of a police officer, all orders to guard the door, all pretenses that he could control someone in my state. He simply looked at me, full of compassion, embodying an open heart. I will never forget how his eyes and his words touched me.

His No, said with intelligent compassion, flawlessly delivered in that moment, saved me from a deeper scar.

This is the fourth level of No. It is the No of honesty. It is the No of recognizing that we are all in this together and that we are here to help each other.

This is the No that makes us honest with ourselves, compassionate with each other, and ready to intelligently, selflessly serve.

This is the No that bridges between the animal and the divine.

This is the No that makes us human.

FORGIVING YOURSELF

As you are going to sleep, take five deep breaths.

Picture someone you are in conflict with. It could be a colleague, a family member, a neighbor, or someone you just bumped into on the street.

At some point it doesn't matter who is right and who is wrong. We are all brothers and sisters here for such a short time. Consider this for a moment while thinking of the other person.

Mentally ask for the other person to forgive you.

Although there is nothing to forgive, picture forgiveness in his or her face. In this way, you are also forgiving yourself, since everything in your imagination is simply a reflection of you.

It's through learning how to forgive yourself that you learn how to speak *truth* to those around you

Truth is a powerful armor. Truth is the primal force behind all of nature, behind all of our needs. Forgive yourself and the power of nature becomes yours.

Say No to Mindless Selfishness

JAMES: Many people say, "Live life like it's your last day."

We get it. Learn to appreciate everything around you. Because it might not be here tomorrow. This is a very important lesson. But it's not what this chapter is about.

Often people take that expression to mean that you should live life without caring. That you can do anything you want because tomorrow might not arrive.

But tomorrow is never lost because it will never exist. It's always today. Try it. Tomorrow when you wake up, where did "tomorrow" go? It's now "today" again.

In fact, you will most likely never know a time when you are not alive.

It's everyone else you need to think about.

This may seem like a silly way to say it, but don't worry. Thinking of it this way could change your life.

Think of someone you love. Or many people you love. Or even people you don't care that much for. What if you got into a fight with one of them? What if they died today?

Here's a new saying to try out. See how this improves the interactions you have today.

"Treat everyone else as if it's *their* last day."

Then you will:

- Be kind to them.

- Try to help them be less stressed.

- Try to fulfill their dreams for the day.

- Not talk badly about them. You don't talk badly about someone about to die.

- Hug them if it's appropriate. Or kiss them. (Not the people I'm going to do business with later. That might be too much.)

- Really listen to them. "I will listen to everyone's last words today without interrupting them. Even if I can finish their sentences because I am light-years ahead of them, I will let them finish their sentences." In fact, not only let them finish what they have to say but show respect. Take a breath and count to two before you respond.

- Learn from them. "I will imagine that some universal life force is speaking to me through everyone else. I will listen carefully for clues that I can decipher later. These are the only clues that God will ever give me so I had better not interrupt."

Each person you interact with is an angel sent down to teach you a lesson. Don't you think you had better listen?

Even though it may sound a little morbid to imagine that people around us are about to die, in reality, this simple mind trick helps us let go of the mindless selfishness that occupies most of our thoughts. If we are lucky, we might even get out of our constant stream of thoughts and notice the human beings around us in a new light and with a disposition to help.

The Strange Things That Happen When You Say No to Lies

JAMES: People tend to think "honesty" somehow depends on "happiness." He can be honest because he is happy or because he has all the money in the world!

But it's not true. Life is a series of failures punctuated by brief successes. That's honesty. Failure is not necessarily bad; it's reality. And even those with all the money in the world still experience heartache, devastation, fear, and death.

We all share the same humanity. On a physical level, there is almost no genetic difference in our DNA between one person and the next.

At a deeper level, we want freedom. Freedom, of course, comes from having our material needs taken care of. But it also comes from having a sense that sometimes the sunset is enough. We don't also need a 40-foot yacht from which to watch that sunset.

Often people are afraid to be honest. "People won't like me" if we say what we think. Or "I might make a fool of myself." Or "I might lose my job." There's an expression: "The pen is mightier than the sword." This simply means that a word of honesty is more powerful than any weapon you can use.

Because the pen—that is, your *word*—is mightier than the sword, faith in the *word* will cause the universe to flow in your direction.

But I must warn you: some unexpected things might pop up. Being true to yourself can and often does result in visible changes in your life. Honesty might even change your friends, your family, and your job. But not everyone may be ready for you to change.

When you start to dip your toes into personal honesty, your family might stop speaking to you. Some of your friends might also stop speaking to you. Some of your colleagues might avoid you.

This is a good sign because it means you are transforming yourself into who you really are, and in turn your personal network/tribe/community will shift and transform.

Our own personal motto is *Honesty to a point.* I will never harm anyone.

The next thing that will happen is people will ask, "Are you killing yourself?" Because everything you say might seem to them like a suicide note. When I first started revealing the most intimate issues of my life that led me to bankruptcy at every level, and how I came back up, people actually asked me if I had had a stroke.

We learn from an early age that life is a costume ball and we have to pick our masks carefully. Entire industries have sprung up to teach people how to manipulate to get what they want.

Ultimately, they miss the fact that whoever needs to manipulate is actually in the weaker position.

With true power you will never be in the weaker position. When you speak from your heart and speak the truth, as difficult as it might be, you do become stronger.

But it's scary. People won't understand what you are doing. They won't understand why you are speaking your mind. Why you are no longer living in the fear that the rest of them live in.

Then people will send e-mails to your friends: "Is he as crazy as he sounds?" And that's how you will meet new friends, because a halo of intrigue and possible integrity will be cast around you.

Over time, other people who are just as special and unique as you are will begin to see you and recognize you from across the room. *Ahhh,* they will think, *someone like me.* And this will be how you find your new tribe. The ones you will grow with.

Still others might get fearful because speaking the truth is intimidating. When people are not ready to get to their own truth, it becomes a challenge to engage with someone who has. So they will call you names. Oh, that guy is just trying to be a "contrarian," for instance. Or an "idiot." Or worse.

It's hard not to take these things personally. Our brains are set to recognize danger before they recognize positivity. But realize that you are now going to be operating at a higher vibration. You don't need to worry about the fears and comments and digs of lower vibrations.

Then, finally, people will come back to you. Because you're entertaining. If 20,000 people are lying and only one person is telling the truth, that one person is going to stand taller than the rest. At first people will come back to you for voyeuristic reasons because they know if they watch *Real Housewives* they aren't watching anything "real" and they aren't watching "housewives." But you're real, so they want to know what you'll do next.

People will also come back for advice because you are a true souce of integrity.

Saying No to a Nervous Breakdown

JAMES: It is not easy for me to be honest. I grew up thinking I had to lie to people to get them to like me. I needed to be someone I wasn't in order to hide the scars I was sure everyone could see.

I thought I had to, for instance, get into a good college for people to like me. Or be a chess master. Or have straight hair. Or get rid of my glasses or my acne. Or have a lot of money.

These were all lies I told myself because I didn't think I could be liked without these medals shining brightly on my shirt.

Then there were lies I told others. I told the first girl I ever went out with that I once stole a lot of money from my parents and lost it all gambling on horses.

Then her dad came to visit, and he heard all about my race-track adventures. He said, "Let's all go to the horse track!" I had never even been to a horse race before. So we went, and I had no idea what I was doing, and it was pretty clear that I had lied to her, as I had on many occasions before that and even after that until there was nothing left of us.

The truth is that I did steal money from my parents. But I spent it all on going to movies and buying comic books and books about chess. And I would use the money to skip school and go into New York and hang out in Washington Square Park and play chess with everyone there. Not an exciting enough story, though, to tell a girl who wanted me to confess all sorts of things to show her what an outlaw I was instead of a Jewish suburban middle-class kid.

Then there are the lies I told as I went from job to job. Skills I had maybe 10 percent of but I claimed 100 percent of. A salary that I would enhance by a few thousand so that when I got an offer I'd make a few thousand more. Titles I had at old jobs that never even existed.

Then later I wouldn't tell people I was getting a divorce. Or losing a home. Or losing hope.

Why did I tell the lies?

I never thought I was good enough for anything. But I always wanted more of it. If I could just get to the fourth rung on the ladder, I was sure the fifth rung had my name on it. And even though I was sweating, hungry, unhappy, and scared, I knew that if I just reached that fifth rung I'd be happy. That the prize was waiting for me there.

So I would lie to get it.

Everyone would forgive me then. Everyone would pat me on the back and have a big meeting and say, "We knew you could do it."

Girls who had broken up with me would claim they were only testing me, that they were also waiting for this moment. They would be side by side with the bosses who had fired me. The people who had ignored me. All of them together in a big party to celebrate me.

They would all be happy, laughing, and slapping me on the back.

But I never reached that rung on the ladder. And I never will. I fell off the ladder instead.

A few months ago I had breakfast with the CEO of a company I once worked for. They had fired me and then withheld a bonus payment I desperately needed. But they had since changed CEOs several times, and now I was meeting their latest CEO, who had reached out to me.

It was around the time they withheld that payment that I realized nobody out there was going to help me. Nobody would be fair. This wasn't a blame thing. Nor was it pessimism. I just needed to pick myself up, and it was my own fault for not dealing with good people. For not constantly being creative. For not feeling grateful.

But in order to be around good people, I also had to be a *real* good person, not an imaginary one. I had to feel abundant without lying about it in order to have abundance hit me. Not in a law of attraction way, but just so I could sleep at night.

It was that simple. I had to stop using all the energy in my brain to come up with imaginary futures. The brain needs a lot of fuel to keep the lies going. Better to use that fuel for being happy and good now than to make up anxieties and regrets for the future.

The CEO said to me, "I heard you had a heart attack or a nervous breakdown a few years ago. That's what everyone told me."

I couldn't believe what she had said. To me I had just had the most fulfilling and successful few years of my life. But to the people who knew me, to people looking in from the outside, it appeared to be a nervous breakdown as every facade fell away. I had been buried in my lies and now I no longer was.

"No," I told her, "I'm healthier than I have ever been."

She repeated, "Everyone insists you had a nervous breakdown."

Maybe I had. But I wasn't nervous. I wasn't broke. And I wasn't down.

Anymore.

—— EXERCISE ——
RECOGNIZING YOUR SHADOW

One of the best ways to get in touch with your real self is to notice those things that you tend to passionately dislike in others.

When you have a moment for reflection, sit down and take a few cleansing breaths. Then think about someone you dislike, and write down the traits in him or her that repel you. For instance, self-righteousness, or carelessness, or passive-aggressiveness.

Recognize that these traits live in you, too. They are the part that you'd rather not look at.

Just by doing this, you can become aware of when you are projecting these qualities onto others. The next time you find yourself criticizing someone for something they do or say, something you feel is very out of line, you will be able to recognize that there is some projection in that. You will also be able to turn it around and ask the question, "Where am I like this?"

This is incredibly powerful and centering. It grounds you to know that you are human and that you share these things you deny so strongly.

Observing the sides of yourself you usually keep in the dark gives you access to power because it grounds you in a more open-minded view of yourself and others.

— FIFTH —

THE NO TO SCARCITY

*You have the right to say no to
the scarcity complex . . .*

JAMES: The power of the alchemist lies not in turning dust into gold. That is a metaphor to show the strength of the mind that lies behind such a miracle.

The real miracle is what happens when in spite of desperation, hurt, defeat, and bankruptcy, we still shift our perception from lack to abundance.

We have our feet on the ground, and we know where we are, but we also trust the infinite force that is keeping us alive right now, and we know we are abundant in this moment, because we are here. How is that for a miracle?

It's fine to be spiritual. It's fine to aim for enlightenment. But let's face it: we have to pay the bills. And in many cases, we're going to have to pay our children's bills for a while, too. And along the way, we're going to get scared. We're going to fear going broke. We're going to fear for our livelihoods. How will our children eat? How will we eat?!

Our brains want us to feel as if the resources of the universe are scarce. For 400,000 years, resources for humans *were* scarce. We had to hunt and gather. But starting only recently in human history, we have been blessed to move beyond this mentality. This phase in our evolution is about abundance instead of scarcity.

To ignore this, to keep living in scarcity, is to reject the next phase in our evolution.

Like anything we do in life, the shift to abundance requires practice. Because it's hard. Yet it's a simple shift. Instead of focusing your perception on what is scarce in your life, try to notice when you feel the grip of scarcity squeeze your heart. Maybe you feel a constriction in your chest. Maybe you get a migraine or feel sick to your stomach.

Maybe you are anxious about a distant future in which all of your needs are not being satisfied. Maybe you are afraid that you are not good enough in some way for your needs to be satisfied.

At this point, you can become an alchemist by feeling the uneasiness and *still* counting your blessings. People say "Count your blessings" as an expression. It's almost a cliché, but clichés exist for a reason: they contain the seeds of truth.

So try it. Count them right now. Count the things you are blessed with. Count your abundance. It could be as basic as counting the people in your life who love you or whom you love. Or it could be dreadfully mundane: you are sitting in traffic, irritated—count the abundant cars in front of you and behind you.

Alchemy happens when we practice again and again noticing the events that point toward doom in the physical world (we lost the job) and yet feel our feelings (open our hearts) and stay with them—we do not let them drown us. We look at them in a neutral way; we invite them for tea. We trust that a resolution is coming.

We know that the brain has our best interests at heart. Nice brain. But (and say it gently), "No, brain."

The reality is that our lives are always abundant, no matter what the past and future look like. The past and the future are dreams, fantasies. Abundance is here right now.

When I (Claudia) returned from my professional yoga training in Thailand in March 2009, I was fired from my job of ten years. I had a mortgage, a car with payments due, $30,000 of debt, and zero savings.

The corporate structure was kicking me out into the night, and it was cold. I literally did not know where I'd be sleeping within the next 30 days. Perhaps because I was just coming from an intense program of breathing, yoga, and meditation every day for an extended period of time, I was especially prepared, and even though I did get scared, I was able to stay with the feelings, remain positive, and accept that what was happening was the exact thing I needed.

And it was.

This does not mean we don't freak out when something difficult happens. We might very well have a couple of "moments," a few days, months, or even years of disorientation. This is being human. If we did not feel anything, we would probably be crazy. And choosing to feel our feelings is not an easy thing.

Sensing a betrayal, injustice, or foul play and feeling it in full without retaliation is hard—especially when we decide to be alchemists and both (a) recognize the part we played in causing the issue and (b) set new boundaries that the circumstances call for. This is the mark of a real warrior. This is what honor is all about. It is owning our choices and our lives.

Just as in the warrior pose of yoga, we stand strong and balanced in the face of the challenge, and as we feel the hamstrings burn, instead of crying, we breathe deeper, adjust our muscles, and do what has to be done to maintain the pose. Of course, we do this within our limits. (We wouldn't force it, as that would hurt us.) But still, we work at finding the elusive middle ground, our edge, and let the air reach it.

The serenity prayer that millions of people recite daily applies very well here, too. Try saying it out loud and see how you feel: *God, grant me the serenity to accept the things I cannot change, the courage to change the things I can, and the wisdom to know the difference.*

— EXERCISE —
THE REVERSE LAW OF ATTRACTION

We've talked about the law of attraction. There are plenty of books, videos, seminars, gurus, astronauts, aliens, angels, and gods who speak of its miracles.

Let's play a different game for a second.

Every time you do a kindness without any hope of credit or return, God cries a teardrop of happiness. So try this:

- Know that your word is good enough to manifest anything you want. The law of attraction, as discussed in many texts, will work for you.

- Know that every day you are entitled to your share of the miracles of that day. In fact, if you trust the universe, miracles will be delivered each day. Coincidences that are not expected. A river that will flow bountifully into an ocean, if you ride with it.

- So say to yourself, *I dedicate today's miracles to everyone else. I want none of them, but I hope everyone else will benefit.*

- Picture all of the people around you enjoying the miracles that were meant for you and living healthier, wealthier, and wiser lives because of those miracles.

- Smile, knowing that the truth you have cultivated has now set everyone else free.

- Begin your day, knowing that you are one of the secret miracle carriers.

Seen in this way, miracles flow through us, and we can recognize the infinite blessings all around us.

Today God sheds a tear, and you set sail on His teardrop. Enjoy.

How to Get Unstuck

JAMES: I felt "stuck" at a corporate job. I had the cubicle. I had the fluorescent lights. I had the boss who could make me cry. I played online chess all day long. I took coffee breaks at 9 A.M., 11 A.M., 2 P.M., and 4 P.M. Since I didn't smoke but wanted to take cigarette breaks with "the guys," I took a pack of licorice with me downstairs and acted tough while they smoked and I ate my candy.

In the morning I couldn't get out of bed. Light would shine in. 7 A.M., 8 A.M., 9 A.M. "Here's some coffee." 10 A.M. Finally, I'd fall over onto the floor. Dog hairs. Cat hairs everywhere. Ugh. All over me. I was three hours late to work. Many days. I was S.T.U.C.K.

I couldn't accurately say I had specific complaints. I had okay colleagues, easy responsibilities. Summers were easy when everyone took a vacation. So what was my problem?

Nothing was my problem.

A lot of people feel stuck. I know this because I get e-mails that start, "I'm stuck." They don't like where they are, but they don't know how to move forward. They don't know how to shake things up. One time a friend told me (he got his Ph.D. at the age of 15, so I believed everything he told me about science) that the way BIC makes lighters is by putting all the parts in a machine and then the machine shakes until the parts somehow all fit together into lighters, and the lighters start falling out.

I don't know if this is true, but I love the idea.

So how do you get "unstuck"? Put all your parts in a machine. Start shaking. It's okay to be stuck; nobody will ever blame you for it. But you'll get less and less happy. Then, in order to get you unstuck, things will start to happen that you didn't intend. Maybe you will have an affair to mix things up. Maybe you'll steal a little from the office. Maybe you'll start to cut corners at work because you've been there long enough to know you can let things slide. You start gossiping too much about the other people. You begin the arduous process of backstabbing to rise up in a world that has teased you into thinking that's how you get unstuck.

But it isn't.

Here's the nine-step guide to getting unstuck:

1. List your routine. Don't leave a single detail out. When you are stuck it means you have a rigid routine. Here was part of mine: wake up, brush teeth, wait for cold subway, ride subway, get a donut and coffee, go to cubicle without anyone seeing me, log on to e-mail, read stuff on the web, play a game of chess, make my list of things to do, start programming . . . flirt . . . gossip . . . lunch . . . coffee break . . . chess break . . . dinner . . . shoot pool, etc. I had about 50 things on my "routine list." Put 60 on yours if you can.

2. Change one thing in the routine. Don't make it too hard. One thing. Don't go straight to work. Go to the library. Or wake up an hour early and read a book. Or jog around the block even if you have never jogged before. Or don't read your e-mails this morning. Or stop gossiping. Or sit with different people at lunch. Over time, how many things on your routine list can you change? Half of them? All of them? Make it a daily challenge. Break your record. Break my record.

3. Write a things-I-did list at the end of the day. The things-I-did list is much better than the standard mainstream tool of productivity: the things-to-do list. Things-to-do is all about stress. I felt like a failure if I didn't check every item on the list.

   Instead, the things-I-did list is one of the few times you can actually use the magic of hindsight to make your life better now. In other words, "Look at this! I actually *did* these things." Pride is a beautiful thing at the end of a hard day. And the list will take on a life of its own. It will be almost like automatic handwriting. You will be surprised at how many things you did. You had forgotten them, but your hands remembered.

   And there they are. On the pad, on the list, written with the pen in your hand.

   Congratulations.

4. Find one thing you were passionate about as a kid; spend an hour researching what has happened in that area since. For instance, I was passionate about Jacques Cousteau. He put out a bunch of books about what goes on underwater. What ever happened to that guy? I couldn't tell you right now if he was dead or alive or buried by some sex scandal. Why do this? Because you were a kid for 18 years. There were probably many things that you were passionate about, even if it was as silly as some cartoon show. Each thing you find out about is something new you learn now. And you might discover things you are still passionate about.

5. Network. Every day find one person to reach out to and stay in touch with. An old high school friend. Somebody you randomly speak to on the subway or on the elevator. Go out to lunch with this person. Learn about his life. Interview him. You need to find out what other routines

are like. Maybe someone will give you an idea you haven't thought of. We are all very afraid to break out of our routines. So am I. I recently agreed to do a media appearance simply because I was afraid that if I said no, the people there would not like me. Reach out to one new person, take a risk, and change something.

6. Create. I can tell by the e-mails I get that most people would rather create something than be a part of the robotic routine. How can you create if you have no time or if you have never done it before? Simple! Don't worry about either of those things. On the subway write a four-line poem. Buy a set of watercolors in the drug store and finger paint for ten minutes before you go to sleep. Don't write a things-to-do list or a things-I-did list. Create a things-I-wish-I-did-today list. Make up stuff for that list. I wish a UFO picked me up, flew me to Andromeda, and then took me home for dinner. It's your wish list for the day that just happened. You can wish for anything. These things didn't happen. The point is that you are making stuff up. You're creating.

7. Daily Practice. Here's why the Daily Practice I recommended earlier works. Remember: that practice is designed to help you get healthy by attending to your physical, emotional, mental, and spiritual well-being every day. This is my personal belief about how the universe is set up. You don't have to believe it, but I know it works for me.

   I firmly believe that we have four bodies and most of the time we neglect at least two or three of them if not all four.

   If you neglect your physical body, you could start to have stomach disorders, you could get sick more frequently, and you could eventually die younger or at least have a painful, unpleasant life. Guess what?

If you neglect your emotional body, you could get depressed, resentful, or angry.

Neglecting your mental body could cause you to be less sharp, less creative, and bitter toward events that seem out of your control.

And if you neglect the spiritual body, you could succumb to a scarcity complex—a belief that you don't deserve anything, a belief that abundance will never come your way.

It's even bigger than that. In your physical body (in all four bodies, actually) there's blood that hooks everything up. If the blood is not working, oxygen is not getting to the different parts of your body. You might have to breathe faster then, or you might breathe irregularly, or worse—if oxygen doesn't get to the heart or the brain then you have a heart attack or stroke. If oxygen doesn't get to your cells properly you get cancer.

And each of your bodies has its own "blood" that holds it all together and keeps it functioning smoothly. Not only that—there's a blood that connects up all four bodies as well. If they aren't all in sync, that blood flow starts to break down.

I know people don't care about all four bodies. They say to me, "I love the idea-muscle idea" or "I like your thoughts but don't really think much about spirituality." This is narrow thinking; it's like saying, "I just need to exercise my legs because I want them to look good."

We need a complete view of our health, and that includes all four bodies.

If *all four bodies* are not in harmony with each other, they begin to break down. You start letting abusive people into your life. Or you start being unable to execute on good ideas. Or you get sick.

Many people don't like certain words, such as *spiritual*. Call it something else, then. Call it gratitude. Call it the compassionate body. The mystery body. Words don't matter.

For me, this is what works. I can't break out of a routine, any routine, unless I am following this advice. So I know it works for me. And I know it works for the people who have heard me talk about this before. I've gotten well over a thousand e-mails on how people's lives have changed. I'm not saying this because I am trying to sell you anything. I'm saying this because it works.

8. What are you afraid of? I'll never get a job this good again. I'll fail as an entrepreneur. I'll run out of money and have to move. I don't know any rich people to help me. On and on. There's excuse after excuse for not breaking your routine, and often excuses are based in fear. You break the routine by being aware of the fears.

Sometimes a "routine" is a person. I wake up . . . did she write to me? It's 11 A.M. . . . has she called? Did she say she loved me yesterday? How come she didn't make plans yet for this weekend with me? She said she would be here at 7 but she hasn't even called, and it's 8 . . . Maybe this routine is particular to me. But ask: What am I afraid of? What in my past might create a routine like this? A parent telling me I was ugly when I was younger. Experiences of other women cheating (she said 7 and now it's 8). Fear that "I will never meet someone like her again" (a statement that is often said but never true). Fear of being alone.

List all the fear excuses. Think about them. Then think of the opposite. Well, I've always met a girl within six months after a big breakup, so I probably will meet one again. Or I haven't lived in a homeless shelter yet so odds are I won't this time.

You might say, "But I really want this girl!" Or "I really might go broke!" That's okay. Think the opposite anyway.

I said I'd offer nine things but I gave you eight. I broke my routine. But that's okay. Oh, wait, here's a ninth: read this chapter again tomorrow.

I eventually climbed out of bed and told my boss I quit. He said, "Can you please wait until I get back from vacation in three weeks?" I said no and sent in my resignation. I eventually stopped calling back "the girl" when it was clear she didn't like me. I eventually stopped gossiping about the people who clearly hated me. I never ended up in a homeless shelter despite being very scared.

Waking up at 7 A.M., lying there until 10 A.M. The sunlight coming in and filling the room when everyone was busy doing their routine and I was too afraid to move. Sometimes I'm still too afraid to move.

But the sun has a way of causing the flowers to blossom, whether they want to or not.

— EXERCISE —
HOW TO BREAK ROUTINES

1. Become aware of the excuses you say to yourself in order to continue with your old routines.

2. Figure out why they exist. What era of your psychological timeline do they come from? What fear do they represent?

3. What's the reverse of that fear? I really had to say to myself, "I will meet a woman I will fall in love with if I leave this relationship." I had to say it over and over. If I didn't say it, I never would've left the relationship. I never would've met the right person (my co-author). If you don't say it, you won't believe it.

4. Don't just say it—see it. Lie down. Put your hands by your sides. Take ten deep breaths. And really visualize the reverse of your fear. In my case I visualized meeting the right person. Feel it as if it were real.

This is how I got unstuck.
Repeat every day as needed.

Saying No to Bad Luck

JAMES: Do you ever say, "I wish I were lucky"?

For instance, if you were in the right place at the right time, you could've met that special someone.

Or if you were Mark Zuckerberg's roommate at Harvard you could be a billionaire.

Maybe you don't want to be a billionaire, but if you hadn't gotten sick right before that audition . . .

And on and on.

We have a love affair with luck.

Sometimes we chase it. Sometimes it teases us. Sometimes we have it for a while. Sometimes when we expect a kiss, it runs away in the rain, leaving us scared and lonely.

Among chess players (and poker players and on Wall Street and often Main Street) there is a saying: "Only the good players are lucky."

Why do they say that? Because people who are cursed with bad luck often lash out: "You only won because you were lucky."

It's a horrible thing, at that point, to be lucky.

"No I am not!" you want to insist.

It's the people who use luck as an accusation who will never have it. You and I will.

Luck is something that is earned, and once you have earned it, you will always know how to get it back. You will say no to the people who try to bring you down, who try to use their own bad luck to control you because they can't climb to your heights.

Luck is the key to freedom. But luck is not magic.

Luck equals (1) diversification plus (2) persistence.

Diversification means coming up with a thousand ideas and implementing the 1 or 2 percent that seem reasonable.

Persistence is a sentence filled with failures punctuated by the occasional success.

Coming up with thousands of ideas means having the energy and creativity to brainstorm.

Energy equals physical plus emotional plus mental plus spiritual health.

All forms of health are a function of how much you control your own life divided by how much people control you.

Ugh. I'm not good with fractions. But basically, if many people control you, then it will be harder to have health, which leads to less energy, which forces you to sacrifice some of your ideas, which results in less diversification.

When I respond to an angry comment, the person who made it controls me. Anger controls me. Then I spend less time being healthy.

If I'm in an unhappy relationship but afraid of the consequences of breaking it, fear controls me.

If I daydream arguments between myself and a boss or a sister or a colleague or whomever, in a sense they are controlling me. In reality, their issues have nothing to do with me.

If I let them control me—or if I try to control them—I sacrifice my health. Then I can't generate ideas. I can't persist. I get unlucky. I lose my freedom.

Every time. No exceptions. I'd rather be healthy than "right."

Learning to Listen
with an Open Heart

When you are speaking with other people, silences are good. Pauses mean love. We want to hear, we are interested, and we care.

Rushing our words means fear. It shows our inability to pay attention, to be present. It reflects that we don't want to let anything in, we must fill in the silences, and we think we know better.

Awkward silences can be good. They contain the chance for new things to happen; they offer a buffer of time for the prewritten scripts we carry in our minds to dissolve and make room for something new.

We (Claudia and James) love silences; we feel embarrassed sometimes, but we respect them anyway. They are vulnerable moments that tell us whether we can be at peace with the person in front of us, even in the absence of words.

We live in a society that speaks way too much; a silence may offer a welcome breath of fresh air.

Try it; you may like it. For the next 24 hours, try giving your full attention to everyone you meet, especially the cashier at the supermarket, the attendant at the dry cleaner's, the people on the elevator or bus. Be there. In silence. With others.

SAY NO TO EXTRA, UNNECESSARY WORDS

The average person speaks 2,500 words a day. See if you can go with 1,200 words today. That is still a lot of words. It could make for a nice day of rest to practice these techniques, whenever you remember them:

- When someone is talking, let him finish.

- Don't say "yeah" in the middle.

- Don't nod your head.

- When someone is finished talking, take a breath.

- Count to two before responding.

- Acknowledge to yourself that real communication doesn't happen in the words; it happens in the silence between the words.

— SIXTH —

THE NO TO NOISE

You have the right to silence and to be fully present, here and now . . .

When you turn on the radio, there's often static between the stations.

Do you know where that static comes from? It's the same static that appears on older TVs when you click between channels.

The static is energy that permeates the universe, and it's left over from the Big Bang.

No joke, that static took 13 billion years to get here, and you can listen to it right now.

But when you get to the right station, the static is gone.

In our lives we are bombarded with noise. Ugly, primal noise. The noise of negativity, the noise of the news that tries to spread its fear, the noise of people complaining about the drudgery and pain of life, the noise of gossip, of manipulation, of aggression.

We all want to tune to the right frequency, the frequency where we have the power to both listen to the music and make the music around us. Where we become our own beacons, our own orchestras.

But you can only do that when you learn to block out the noise.

IDENTIFYING THE NOISE

Start to identify the static/negative noise around you:

- News that tries to scare you

- Gossip

- People putting you or others down

- Negative thoughts of worry or regret

- Fears and anxieties about the future

- Angry thoughts

In this exercise we don't need to act on anything. It's very hard sometimes to pay attention to the things we do that harm us, but learning to notice the noise is a good first step.

Your Purpose . . . Now

JAMES: The goal is not to eliminate the noise; that's impossible. Just like it's impossible to stop the static that emanates to this day from the Big Bang that created the entire universe. It's always in the background.

But being aware of the noise and its mighty destructive power will help you transform it into a just-as-mighty positive power in your life.

We choose what information we let in, and we choose how we communicate. We use our words carefully, aware of their power, for words cast spells, no question about it.

We realize there is a divine plan for all of us, and we are willing to listen.

Note: this does not mean listen for a booming voice that says "Moses, go free the slaves!" You will spend many sleepless nights if you are listening for that voice.

It's not that you don't have a lifelong goal or a purpose, but you also have a purpose right now: to simply cut out the noise so the divine whispers can come in. The higher power that has our backs, the one we sensed intimately in the fourth No, and maybe way before then, wants to be in touch with us every day. And we find it in the only place where it can be found: in the silence.

From the silence we move toward a higher-frequency life, one that we live as if it were a prayer. We lead lives that teach by example, that show instead of tell. Lives that add instead of detract.

We become the change we want to see in the world, as a great listener named Gandhi once said.

A story: A woman came to Gandhi and asked if he would please tell her son to stop eating sugar, to which he said yes, only he would do it the next week, so she should bring the boy back in seven days.

The woman, who would have to take a long trip twice now, and for no apparent reason, understandably asked upon her second arrival why he had not just gotten it done earlier. Why did she have to come back? Gandhi said it was because *he* had to stop eating sugar before asking anyone else to do so.

He had to make sure his own word was pure and true. That he was on the right frequency and not just emitting the noise of countless gurus with conflicted goals and ideas. How is that for being the change?

— EXERCISE —
CHANGE THE CONVERSATION

You've already begun to notice the noise around you.

Now when you notice the noise, change the conversation. If there is bad news on the TV, turn the TV off.

If someone is gossiping, move away or change the discussion.

If the negative thoughts in your head start whispering of regret or anxiety or worry, stop yourself and replace them with gratitude and thoughts of abundance.

Worry has never once solved a future problem but it will always steal away your strength today.

The power to change the conversation is not just about two people talking. It's about the constant hum of a planet that is always talking, always worried, always filled with regret and anxiety.

If you consistently do the following four steps, you will develop the powers to make that change.

1. Notice when you are in pain, feeling negative or anxious or worried or regretful or angry or scared. You might feel these things in your head. You might feel them in your body. Maybe your chest hurts, or your stomach, or your back.

2. Ask yourself, "Why? What is causing this pain? Am I worried about events I have no control over? Am I worried about a future that probably will never come true? Do I feel bad about something I said ten years ago?" You can't change these things; just identify them.

(continued on following page)

3. Stop. That's it. Just stop. If it helps, look around. Be grateful for the beauty in your life. Be grateful for anything good that is happening right now in either your life or the world.

4. Take a step back. This very day, this very second, are you promoting your health in the following ways?
    Physical: Doing the best you can to promote physical health.
    Emotional: Being with the people you love. Being with the people who inspire you.
    Mental: Coming up with ideas to help people.
    Spiritual: Expressing gratitude. Acknowledging that you can't control everything in the world.

Changing the conversation means changing your life, which changes the lives of the people around you, which changes the entire universe. This attracts abundance and success into your life as the universe changes itself to hear your words.

Speak softly, because you carry a big stick.

The Ultimate Secret to Raising Your Vibration

CLAUDIA: "You need to sit for two hours today," I heard myself saying in my head. It was an intense day—I had a radio appearance in the evening and a book deadline—yet the message I was receiving about my daily hour of silence was to sit for *two* hours?

I did, of course, and it was exactly what I needed.

I sit in silence every day. I almost never skip. The only times I am unable to do it come when we are traveling and speaking, when the demands on my nervous system are already too strong. On those days I listen to a relaxation tape for one hour.

This practice dates back to one April a few years ago when I spiraled down into a depression that took hold of my body, mind, and spirit. I was upset and confused.

By late spring the fire of rage in my belly had made a violent U-turn, and I was the one burning.

When anger is turned inward, it results in depression. Anger and depression are like the mirror cravings of a lonely soul.

We visited an Eastern medicine practitioner in New York City. He took my pulse, looked at my tongue, and prescribed herbs to lift my energy and make my heart happy. What surprised me was how he involved me directly and permanently in the healing process. This was not about taking a pill and leaving the cure up to him; it was about owning my health.

Then he said, "Claudia, you must sit in silence for one hour a day."

Silence! This is his advice? To me? The so-called yogi? The one who endured not one, but two brutal ten-hour-a-day meditation courses and a series of meditation retreats, including an attempt (admittedly failed) at a week of solitude in a forest cabin? My ego was in denial—it did not want this.

Naturally, I asked: "Can I do thirty minutes in the morning and thirty in the evening?"

"No! You sit. For one hour. All at once. Every day. Be silent, and let your thoughts go. Do it," he said.

I was not sure I *could* do it. I had tried this kind of practice many times after the momentum of retreats, and I always ended up giving it up. I had read all the best yoga books, and it just wasn't working for me. Let's face it, the reality was that I didn't want to do it.

He sensed what I was thinking, I guess, because he said, "I have another patient who has cancer. I told him to sit for eight hours of silence a day. I said to him, 'You want to heal? You sit for eight hours.'"

After that I couldn't argue. I knew I had to do it.

I understood that this was not yoga or meditation—this was different. Silence was not a goal or something to attain. I was sick and silence was medicine. As I sat there looking at him, in tears, full of doubt, and seeing that he would not let me go unless we had an agreement, I nodded. Up and down. Not happy but in full understanding.

I have been sitting in silence for one hour a day ever since.

Sit in silence for as long as you like, every day, because silence works.

Nobody can teach anyone how to do this. I've been to the edges of the world and beyond looking for teachers, for some-one who would show me the right way. There is no such person. I've been to spiritual retreats in South America, Europe, the U.S., Canada, India, Thailand, all in the spirit of the quest.

I've learned lots of pointers, and they all come back to one thing—sit in silence: let it happen, let yourself drip into this moment just as you are, in complete acceptance. If emotions appear, let them. Then release them. That's it. When we release an emotional issue instead of getting all wrapped up in it, we help the issue lose its power over us.

Of course, when I sit, I am not always calm and poised, and the techniques and exercises come in handy.

Let me tell you about some of these tools, borrowed from yogis who have been experimenting for thousands of years with how to sit in silence, how to quiet the mind, and how to heal by using their energy in a more effective way.

HOW TO DEEPEN THE SILENCE
AND REAP THE REWARDS

Grounding: This is an excellent and well-kept secret that yogis use to center and gather their energy so they can sit and quiet the mind.

Picture a two-way street going up and down your spine: one lane goes toward the center of the earth and the other one into the infinite universe up above.

As you inhale slowly and your chest fills with air and expands, counterintuitively, focus on the root of your body, the area of the perineum, and all the way down to the center of the earth.

Then, as you exhale and the body deflates and its energy tends to go down, you picture your mental energy flowering up like a lotus and expanding into the universe through the top of your head.

By stretching the imagination in the way opposite of the way the breath is flowing, yogis send vital energy to all parts of the body. This helps with being present, because the more we feel the body, the more we let the mind go.

There is no need to repeat it many times. Just a few slow breaths with these visualizations will serve to ground your energy and calm your mind.

Being with it: Old feelings will appear when you sit in silence. This is an opportunity to clear them up, to let them go. Welcome them; they are here to be released. Observe them and know they cannot make you feel miserable or happy for very long. Like every wave of life, they will rise and fall. Let them be. Then let them go.

When you do this, when you observe long-pent-up feelings coming up and then leaving, without reacting, they lose their power over you, and you become freer.

Flushing the lungs: This is a simple one. Just exhale, and then when you are done exhaling, exhale some more, then more, then more. You will find you have no more air whatsoever. Then the inhale will feel good. Enjoy it.

Flushing the subconscious: On days when I feel like taking an entrepreneurial approach to my silence, I try the yogic exercise of painting a tomato can–sized black dot in the center of a blank page and staring into it without blinking (a technique known as *trataka*).

When your eyes begin to water, you close them and hold on to the image. This exercise flushes things out of your subconscious. Use it carefully; it might stir old memories. But it might also ventilate them.

Respecting the process: Do not get attached to any particular feeling or result. Just as each snowflake is unique, everyone's process is different.

Respect anything that happens in the time allocated to silence.

Skull-shining exercise: This tool is especially helpful for those days when the mind just will not stop. I have found it to be the *most powerful* technique ever downloaded by yogis to switch the mind from one state to another. From overactivity, to less activity, to silence. And it works because it completely and immediately changes the breathing pattern.

The only thing is that it is important to do it right because otherwise it can hyperventilate the brain and make you dizzy, or it just won't work. It is also not recommended for people with high blood pressure. It might be wise to consult a professional before attempting this one.

This exercise is also known in yoga circles as *kapalabhati,* Sanskrit for "skull shining."

(continued on following page)

1. Make sure you have a very empty stomach (no food in the past four to five hours).

2. Sit in a comfortable position, cross-legged or on a chair with both feet on the floor (not lying down, because it will not be as effective). Posture is important, so for this practice, take a moment to check it.

   Straighten your back, but don't overdo it; respect your body.

   Relax your hips.

   Tilt your pelvis slightly forward.

   Open your chest.

   Roll your shoulders back but without forcing them.

   Relax your jaw, palate, and face. It will feel good.

   Take one deep breath and exhale saying Aaaahhhhh as a sigh of relief.

   Smile internally.

3. The actual exercise consists of inhaling halfway, then forcefully exhaling from the belly, then repeating. There is no forcing on the inhale—you only force the exhale, the inhale happens naturally. The mistake some people make is to force the inhale, too. Don't do that.

4. Try to move only your belly (not your arms, your shoulders, or your face). Proceed slowly, doing one forceful exhale at a time.

5. Check again to make sure your face is relaxed. Making faces is a funny mistake people make.

6. Do it again. Take your time. In the beginning you may get only six or seven relaxed forceful exhalations before you lose your rhythm.

7. Losing your rhythm means you are ready to stop. It is important to stop then, pause, and maybe do another round once you recover your composure, or wait until the next practice.

8. Let it grow on you—both the number and speed of your exhalations—over days and months. It took me four weeks of daily practice to build up to 30 *kapalabhati* breaths, but everyone is different, so do take your time (say no to rushing!). Doing just a few will have a great calming effect on your mind. Building up to 30 and then more will have a much deeper effect.

When you are sitting in silence, if you are distracted, you may remember one of these exercises. Then you can try it. But the really necessary thing is to simply sit. These are just aids. They are not meant to be practiced or learned all at once.

If you feel that impulse, notice that you are veering away from the important thing, which is to sit in silence and just be. To take your time. To return to stillness.

We Are Not
Our Thoughts

CLAUDIA: I wish I could really get that I am not my thoughts.

Many of us have a big hurt in our emotional body. And I am not talking about a cheap drama; I mean a real hurt. A deep wound. The one we tend to avoid, or pretend was no big deal, or keep secret.

Last fall I had the enormous opportunity of meeting Thich Nhat Hanh in New York City. It was a warm evening, and a group of people had gathered at a very fine furniture store in Manhattan.

Deepak Chopra introduced Thich Nhat Hanh as "a person who embodies peace." And we could feel how true that introduction was as soon as he stepped onto the stage, surrounded by his entourage of monks and nuns.

The first thing he said was that the nuns and monks were to sing to us. This was different from what I expected, which was something like a lecture or a talk, but somehow in his presence it all made complete sense.

At first, said Thich Nhat Hanh, the monks and nuns would connect with their own inner pain to access compassion and chant to us a song. What a great way of accessing compassion! I had never noticed it, but when I feel pain, then I can relate to the pain of others.

Then, he continued, they would sing the same song again, only this time, after feeling and connecting to their own pain, they would send all the "mother love" they had in them toward us in the audience.

This made me a bit uncomfortable. I wondered if all the love that these nuns and monks had would be overwhelming for a sensitive person like me. So I took one deep breath and stayed with the experience, open to whatever might come.

When they sang the first time, my heart ached in a profound way. I remembered the recent death of my father, and I lost it. And I was not the only one—many women and some men, I noticed, were crying with me.

It felt as if a sense of human connection was arising in the audience. We were not presenter and listener anymore; we were all one, connected by the humanity we share, by the nervous systems we all have with their painful memories, by our minds, bodies, and hearts.

When the monks and nuns moved on to the second round of singing and directed the mother's love to us, all my discomforts over wearing very high heels that night disappeared. I don't know why I wore them. Maybe because I thought that all Buddhist gatherings involved sitting down and taking shoes off. Maybe because it was fashion week and I had to feel fabulous.

In spite of standing on them, I felt uplifted, comforted, and contained. As shallow as the shoes seemed to my mind, in truth all of my emotional body felt uplifted.

And you could see the vulnerability in the audience and feel the specialness of the moment.

A few people in front of me were taking videos and photos on their phones, even though we had been told at the entrance not to do that. But I understand why they did it. Seeing it all through the screen puts a veil in front of the feeling. It puts distance between us and what is happening. It puts time between the actual experience of what is happening and having to feel it. It helps to avoid crying and embarrassment. It is a defense mechanism.

But many other people in the audience stayed with it. And, in doing that, they allowed the emotional wounds to surface, to show that we hurt, and that we are not alone. We all hurt. We could feel it right in that space, our common hurt. That is compassion. Thich Nhat Hanh was not telling us about it; we were experiencing it, living it, with him. He was showing us.

As the second round of chanting continued, most of us in the audience allowed ourselves to find the beginning of the thread toward emotional healing. We knew we had to. It's our responsibility.

Without being whole in our emotional bodies, it is difficult to be of service to others. If we don't heal we can't help heal anyone else. It hurts too much. It is easier to escape, to not look, to find another person to have sex with, or drink one more glass of wine.

When the monks and nuns retired for the evening, James and I walked through the exhibition of paintings that Thich Nhat Hanh had made especially for the event. One read, "Flow like a river." Another one said, "No mud, no lotus." One was funny—it said, "To be or not to be is no longer the question."

The last one I saw read, "One Buddha is not enough."

I wish I were like a Buddha. I wish I knew that I am *not* my thoughts. But the way toward knowing that, the way to stop identifying with the constant stream of thinking that stops me from seeing reality, starts by healing my own wounds. I must stop, find a nice cave, and tend to them.

It is in the silences that our deepest caves get flooded with universal light.

My deep wound gives me plenty of mud from which, when the time is right, a lotus may blossom.

The Benefits of Silence

JAMES: Many people define *minimalism* as "not needing material things," so they obsessively reduce the material things in their lives.

There is nothing wrong with this. And, in fact, it may work to make life simpler. The key is to be careful that your definition of minimalism doesn't border on a sort of material anorexia, where you deny yourself the small celebrations that life wants you to have.

A more holistic way to practice minimalism is to look not only at your physical surroundings but also at your "noise surroundings": the noises you hear, the sounds you speak, the thoughts that are louder than actions.

The space inside of us is enormous. It's infinite. Keeping this space clean and fresh is true minimalism.

There are many benefits to this form of silence. And they range from the material to the spiritual. From abundance to magic.

- **Professionalism.** This comes up in all forms. Doctors don't talk about patients. Attorneys cite attorney-client privilege. Psychiatrists don't gossip about what they've heard from the couch.

    Silence is the sign of a professional. You even see it in the movies. The gruff hit man who doesn't talk about what he's seen on the job. The soldier who won't talk about the war.

You know not to ask a professional what he's working on. What he's seen. It's in his world and part of who he is and how he moves and expresses himself.

Her silence is the top of the pyramid. Her vast experience is everything that lies underneath.

- **Trust.** Other people trust the woman or man who knows how to be silent. Who knows how to keep a secret. Who doesn't gossip.

  One time a friend of mine was gossiping at work about another woman she worked with—call her Diane. Diane overheard her, and my friend was horrified.

  She did all the right things afterward. She apologized to Diane. She was extra nice to Diane. She gave credit to Diane and acknowledged her in meetings and in the hallway and at work functions.

  "Diane is still mad at me!" she said to me almost a year later. "Why would she be mad at me? I apologized. I gave her those references. I always help her. Why?"

  Because you weren't silent, so she doesn't trust you. And she never will again.

- **Value.** Remember this equation: the value of words = the demand for those words divided by the supply of the words.

  Assuming the demand for your words basically stays the same (who wakes up thinking, *I have to hear James and Claudia talk?*) the less supply you give of your words and wisdom, the greater value that wisdom will have.

  I am not making this up. Try it.

  One time I was at a job I was planning to leave, so I simply stopped talking in meetings because I didn't care anymore.

The next thing I knew, they were offering me the CEO position (which I rejected). That's how sharply the value of my words went up when I stopped speaking.

- **Time saved.** The less time you speak, the more time you have for other endeavors. Like listening, reading, exercising, or even sleep. I'd much rather sleep than speak.

- **Mystique.** Ever notice the cool guy or girl at the party is often the one standing in the corner looking at everyone else? I am not advising that you be silent in order to create an aura of mystique. That seems rather narcissistic.

  Yet this is what will happen. In the land of the blind, the one-eyed man is king. When everyone spills their guts, they lose their sight. The one who holds on to this very precious resource becomes the one-eyed man, the king.

- **Observation.** When you are not talking or incessantly chattering in your mind, you observe. You see what's around you.

  Sometimes what you see is just beauty that you can observe and appreciate. Outside my window right now is a tree on which the leaves have turned a bright yellow, leaving tears of yellow underneath it, while lush green trees on either side protect their dying sister.

  Sometimes what you see is keen observation that will help you later—whether it's the words in a book, the tells of a poker player, the inner radiance of a monk, or just the frowns and worries of a friend who needs your compassion.

- **More brain energy.** Your brain, digestive system, heart, and lungs all keep you alive and they need energy. When you talk a lot, the brain needs more energy. It has to keep a conversation going. That's hard work!

The less you talk, the more the brain conserves its energy for when words are important. Don't forget that words are just tools to survive. They aren't you. They don't define you unless you let them.

- **Less web to untangle.** "Oh what a tangled web we weave" goes the famous line. How does it get so tangled? And how do we weave it? By talking.

   And all of this applies to inner talking as well. The silence of just sitting and being comfortable with yourself cuts through these webs before you have a chance to tangle them.

- **Less stress.** Raise your hand if you've ever woken up the morning after a party and thought, *Oh my God—I can't believe I said that.* Go ahead. I won't tell anyone. Raise your hand.

   That's one type of stress. But talking causes many types of stress. We've already looked at many examples so I won't repeat them here.

   And we all know the negatives of stress. But there are some positives, too. Stress can be a warning sign to not do certain things again. Or a sign that we need to get some things done.

   But these are mild benefits of stress. Most people live in a constant state of fight or flight. The trouble is that in our sedentary society, most people aren't moving. They aren't fighting and they aren't "flighting," so stress becomes a killer. It causes heart attacks, strokes, stomach ailments, cancers, Alzheimer's, and on and on.

   So yes, listen to your stress to see where it's pointing you. But don't create mindless stress with mindless talking. Say no to that.

When you say no to the noise and welcome in every layer of silence, you say yes to a healthier life. A happier life.

Why Does the Buddha Love Saying No?

JAMES: At first glance, it doesn't sound good.

A rich playboy, son of a king, gets everything he wants whenever he wants it. Then he gets a beautiful bride, the best of all his choices.

On the night he has a son, he becomes terrified of responsibility so he gets on a horse and leaves his home, abandoning his responsibilities as an heir, a husband, and a father.

Then eight years later he comes back. Surprise!

When he leaves again, against the begging of his father and wife, he takes his son with him.

The man I describe, of course, is Siddhartha Gautama, later known as the Buddha.

Of course, times were different then. Siddhartha knew that a support system was in place to provide for his family and kingdom. He also had a greater calling, one that took years to realize.

What did he finally come to realize?

That he no longer had to say yes.

His father had tried so hard to protect him. Just like the brain tries to protect us. Tries to keep us in our comfort zone so that nothing scary or disruptive happens.

Siddhartha's father was told that his son would be either a great king or a great spiritual teacher who would help alleviate people's suffering, so he tried to prevent his son from seeing any suffering. He kept him locked within the castle, with every plea-sure at his disposal.

But Siddhartha finally saw suffering on his first trip out into the kingdom he ruled.

The mind wants us not to see the suffering that is out there.

But Buddha said no to this self-deception.

He said, "Life is suffering." This is not pessimism. It's not the opposite of positive thinking. It's reality. We get sick. Our jobs and friendships and relationships go up and down. Our anxieties and regrets come back again and again. And we grow old and undergo all the pains and troubles that come with that.

He said, "Suffering comes from craving." We often grow up thinking, *If I get a college degree, if I get a good job, if I get a home where I can establish roots, if I get a great spouse and have kids, if I make a lot of money,* then *I can be happy.*

Maybe you don't think all of those things—not everyone does. But you probably think of some variation of them, and I don't blame you. It's nice to have a great spouse, or kids, or a good job. No one is saying it isn't.

It's the disappointment that happens when you don't get those things that kills you.

There are two arrows in life that try to harm you. Be careful!

Let's say you don't get a job you want. That's the first arrow. That arrow probably won't kill you, but it will cause pain.

But then you start to wonder why. You start to regret. You start to get anxious: *What if I* never *get a job?* You think and you think and you think.

That's the second arrow.

And it *can* kill you.

Buddha's second precept explains the second arrow. Craving is suffering.

But he also said, "There is a way out of suffering."

I like how he throws that in there, and we all lean in a little closer. What is the way out of craving so we don't have to suffer?

And then he tells us the way: meditation, mindfulness, and his eight noble truths.

Let's describe his approach by getting back to the story. Let's skip the eight noble truths and the meditation for a second.

One time, after the Buddha's son, Rahula, joined him on his journey, the Buddha took him for a walk. He gave his son fatherly advice.

This is the last mention of Rahula in any Buddhist text, but perhaps it is the most important.

Let's call it "Buddha explains the Power of No to his son."

All he said was this: "Before, during, and after you think, say, or do anything, determine if it will harm someone."

That's it.

Should you gossip about that co-worker who backstabbed you? No. Then you would be saying something that harms someone.

Should you buy that house? Possibly. But is there a chance it could bankrupt you and your family and put you into massive debt that can only be paid off if you work 80 hours a week and miss your children growing up? Then no.

Should you drive a car? Well, there is a chance you could hurt someone. So you'd better be a good driver and make sure you focus while driving.

The driving a car example is important. You could certainly hurt someone. But use discernment. If while driving you follow "right action" as Buddha would call it, you won't hurt anyone.

But what about buying a house? What if I follow right action when I do that? Okay, then buy it. But don't go bankrupt and go into foreclosure later.

He's not saying, "Say yes to the things you want to do so you can be happy."

He's saying, "Say no to the things that may harm you."

And as the Buddha also said, "Don't take my word for this. Try for yourself. See if this works for you."

Saying No to Incoming Negative Energies

People often try to provoke us. They want a response. They are lonely, and they need us to be angry or upset or scared or ashamed so they won't be as lonely. And it's easy to fall into their traps. To get sucked into the vortex of negativity.

This is not a one-time thing. Or something that happens once a month or once a year. It happens every day. We get sucked into the negativity by having a simple phone conversation, or watching the news, or watching the events on the street.

It's so easy to feel the negativity everyone feeds upon.

The key is to notice it, notice when it starts to well up in your head.

Then stop it. Say no to it.

The only way to do this is to exercise the gratitude muscle.

When you are grateful, in place of negativity, suddenly you see the subtleties in everything around you. Suddenly you notice the coincidences that appear in your life. Suddenly you appreciate the empty spaces that magically appear in a once all-too-crowded world.

— EXERCISE —
GIVING GRATITUDE A WORKOUT

List on a paper all the problems in your life. For example:

1. I lost my job with a bad boss.

2. I can't get a job.

3. Every creative act I do is rejected.

4. My girlfriend/boyfriend cheated.

5. My house is in foreclosure.

6. I'm working as a bartender even though I really want to be acting or writing a novel.

7. I work as a janitor when in my old country I used to be a doctor.

8. My neighbor is too loud!

9. The IRS is after me.

And so on.

You're not going to love these situations; saying you do is a false spirituality. It's also ego—as if you have the power to force yourself to love something that you really, deep down, hate. And to try and fill these situations with love can damage the spiritual muscle rather than build it.

To practice positive thinking on legitimately bad situations will only make you more stuck. It will only continue to separate you from reality.

(continued on following page)

The goal is to be tranquil about the bad situations now. And you can only do that if you start being grateful for the things in your life that you feel are actually good.

Start somewhere, at some baseline. *I love my wife and two daughters, and I'm grateful for them.* Okay, that's a big thing. Start with something smaller. *I'm grateful that I am breathing right now.* You have to start somewhere, even if it's just being grateful for breathing.

When you practice being grateful, when it becomes second nature to you, it becomes easier to say no to situations that you think will make you happy but will only end up causing you misery.

And most important, you will suddenly be "unstuck." In fact, you will realize that you were never "stuck" in the first place because of all the abundance in your life that you are grateful for.

That awareness, which is so easy to implement in your life, is the foundation by which all miracles are built.

So let's put it together. Here's how you exercise the gratitude muscle:

1. List all the negative situations in your life.

2. List the good situations in your life so you don't take them for granted. I'm very grateful for my children, for instance.

3. Try this (it's hard): be grateful, all day, for everything you look at, no matter how small. These things are all here with you right now. It's okay to be thankful for the small things in life.

4. Try this: go on a Gratitude Diet. For the next ten days, when you wake up, think of ten things you are grateful for. They can be important things (family and friends, for example). Or they can be small things (the sun is out). The universe, after all, is a collection of tiny particles. Practicing being grateful for the smallest particles in your life is a good message to send to the universe.

—SEVENTH—
THE NO TO "ME"

You have the right to surrender . . .

"No me?" I hear you say?

Yes. That is what we mean. There is no you, and there is no me. There is only one of us here.

At higher levels of awareness No means "clear discrimination." Discrimination is the fountain from which we drink.

We use the force of discrimination to see when we are being pulled by the ego into chatter, jealousy, and judgment, or instead, when we are being directed by the divine toward what needs to be done through our talents and what we feel is *our calling*.

We are all invited, expected, and wanted here. There is fresh air at the top of the mountain. The delusions have vanished, our energy is well directed, we are fully alive and filled with creativity, and our efforts result in powerful actions in the world that bring us deep satisfaction.

Our talents serve humanity; our directives come from the silence.

We can't say yes until we experience the deepest No.

At this level we do not pay attention to or worry about what others think. We are independent of the good or bad opinions of others. We are free because we know, from the magma of wisdom pouring out of the daily silence and our spiritual rituals, that we must do our best work. And we love it.

We are flowing gently down the river of divine wisdom, on purpose, detached from outcomes, fully trusting and smiling.

The Ultimate No

Surrendering in order to live a life directed by divine forces is the ultimate goal of a person whose energy has risen.

Inhale. The entire world. Everything. All of your past. All of your future.

Exhale. It's gone.

You have arrived.

Welcome.

Does Surrender
Mean Giving Up?

Sometimes we can't handle it anymore.

The debts. The relationships that slap us in the face. The business opportunities that just don't go through, again.

How many times are we supposed to put up with it?

Sometimes we think, *Wow, has it been X years since Y happened?* where Y was some mystical good thing that made us happy.

And then we think, *I've worked every minute of these past few years and what do I have to show for it?*

We feel like giving up.

That's the thought, as in an exasperated, "I give up!"

Is this surrender?

No.

It's the opposite.

It's based on the illusion that you ever had control in the first place.

Here are some of the things you have no control over:

- The weather

- Yesterday's weather

- Which people will like you and hate you

- The moment of your death

- Actually, the moment of your birth, too

- The opportunities that may or may not appear in front of you

And the list goes on.

Well, what is surrender, then?

Can we just say, "Okay, *you* take care of it. *You* do it all," where "you" is some higher power, some godlike entity?

That doesn't work either. If you do nothing, usually nothing happens. This is just a more insidious way of trying to control things. It's like you are trying to passive-aggressively guilt-trip the universe into providing for you.

Surrender is something else. If you've reached this point, if you've said no to all the things you are entitled to say no to, you are ready to *surrender*.

But not before then.

Surrender means:

- You are eating well.

- You are sleeping well.

- You are taking care of your body.

- You are saying no to the foods and drinks and activities that can harm you.

- You are saying no to the people who are trying to bring you down.

- You are saying no to the stories that people have tried to force you into. You are not marching in the army; you are your own person.

- You are saying no to the lies that keep the stories going.

- You are saying no to the offers and opportunities that might be second best. You are searching deeply for the real Yes in the opportunities that come to you.

- You are saying no to the noise. Finding the silence that is between every word, that is between every breath of air.

All of this allows your creativity to roam free. Your spirit to relax. Your brain to breathe a sigh of relief. Your body to have more energy than ever.

So much relief!

Now . . .

Surrender.

To whom?

To you.

To the higher part of you.

To the "you" that is wise and *knows better*.

Do it.

Say yes.

To you.

THE ALIEN TECHNIQUE
FOR SURRENDERING

This is best tried in the early morning.

You wake up.

Your first thought of the day is *Who am I?*

Because you know, deep down, you are an alien from outer space.

You were sent here by the mother ship to inhabit this body for 24 hours. You have no idea who the body is or what you are supposed to do in this body.

Flex your muscles a little bit. Are you a human? What lights are coming into the room? What sounds can you hear?

Is there any part of your body that's feeling a little sick? It might be a sign that this human is suffering from some undue stress.

Your job might be to solve that stress.

Ahh, light is coming in. You soak it up. People from your alien race like light.

Whatever you do today, you know you will help the human; that is why you are here. You know you will make the right decisions for her or him.

But it doesn't matter that much. Because tomorrow you will wake up in another human body. You are a special agent.

And your job is to save lives.

Surrendering Is
a Funny Thing

It almost seems as if these exercises are ways to trick you into surrendering control over the things you cannot control.

And it's true. They are tricks. Because your mind doesn't want to surrender.

Your brain has been given a huge evolutionary responsibility to take care of everything, keep you alive, and put you in the best position possible to replicate your DNA.

It doesn't realize that in just the very recent past we've gone from being the hunter-gatherers we were for millions of years (if you include our evolutionary ancestors) to having the problems of a relatively affluent, technologically sophisticated society.

Our ideas have evolved much faster than our brains have. We can now travel around the entire world in a day. We can watch images from around the world without the span of a second going by. We can eat a meal made up of foodstuffs that have been ploughed, hunted, gathered, processed in maybe 50 different locations around the world, and transported to us so we don't go hungry that day.

We have created a wonderful world to live in, yet we are desperately unhappy. I am not saying you are, but people in general. We've invented antidepressants, and they are among the most profitable drugs in history for a reason.

Our brains don't care if we are happy. There is *only one mission for the brain:* replicate the DNA.

When DNA doesn't replicate, a species becomes extinct. That's failure. When DNA replicates, a species thrives. That's success.

And that's all the brain knows. So we have to get the brain out of the way. We have to trick it or hypnotize it.

Meditation, or simple silence every day, does that. But there are many ways to do it. Just following the ideas in this book will do it.

The brain requires an enormous amount of energy every day, every second, to do what it does. Ultimately, by clearing the deck and using that energy in more productive ways, you can surrender to the energy. Because the pure energy knows what to do, if you trust it.

When you go on a long trip, you see the road in front of you. You trust that if you stay on that road, you will get to where you need to be. You don't try to see the end of the road. You give up control. You surrender to the fact that the road knows better than you what is at the end of it.

That doesn't mean the road will carry you. *You still have to take each step.*

Reading this book is one step. We, the authors, thank you for reading it. We know the ideas in it will help you because they have helped us and many of our readers over the years.

Every time you say no in the way you are entitled to, it will help you take a step forward on this road. But the highest No you can say is to everything you once thought was the being known as "you." Your history, your upbringing, your things, your dramas, your relationships. Those are all your story, and you have to give up control of that story.

You took the first step on your road when you were born. And now here you are.

Go take another step. And another. You don't know where you will end up, but wherever you go, there you are.

SAYING YES TO YOUR NEW POWER

JAMES: You are reading this book because the word *no* rang true to you. Because you are aware that you have a gift to give this world, and that the world is now ready for the energy you are here to deliver. But you need a plan—a map to reinvention.

This is the skeleton of that plan. Follow it and you will see miracles, success, and abundance in your life. I've seen it work for hundreds of people. Through interviews, through people writing us letters, through people attending our workshops, through the course of the past 20 years. You can try it or not.

The list that follows is the crème de la crème of all the questions and comments I've received over the years. It is the fruit of seeing what works and what does not.

As with all condensed forms of information, there is a lot here. You may want to take your time with it. Read a few today, and another few in a few days. Go back to the drawing board whenever you need to. There is no rush.

Reinventing ourselves is bound to send us back to the drawing board again and again, as we grow up, get married, have children, fulfill our lives with work that enriches us, and grow older and wiser.

Everyone experiences the need for reinvention throughout his or her life. Maybe you lose a job. Or a relationship. Or you find a new passion. Or you find new love in your life.

Reinvention takes many forms. It's like Halloween. The doorbell is constantly ringing. There's always someone outside with a new disguise on. They want you to feed them and laugh with them.

Reinvention is ringing at your door all the time.

It is ringing right now.

The Road Map to Reinventing Yourself

a) *Reinvention never stops.*

Every day you reinvent yourself. You're always in motion. But you decide every day whether it's forward or backward.

b) *You start from scratch.*

Every label you claim from before is just vanity. You were a doctor? You were Ivy League? You had millions? You had a family? Nobody cares.

You lost everything. You're a zero. Don't try to say you're anything else.

c) *You need a mentor.*

Or you'll sink to the bottom. Someone has to show you how to move and breathe. But don't worry about finding a mentor (see below).

d) *There are three types of mentors.*

Direct: Someone who is in front of you who will show you how he or she did it. What is "it"? Wait.

Indirect: Books. Movies. You can outsource 90 percent of mentorship to books and other materials. Two hundred to 500 books equal one good mentor. People ask us, "What is a good book to read?" and we never know the answer. There are 200 to 500 good books to read. Start with one, follow the recommendations for further reading in the back of *that* book, keep going, and add different topics— self-help, inspirational, individual to your area of work, and so on. Whatever your beliefs may be, follow your passions and see where they lead you. Underline them through reading every day. Note the passages that really stand out for you.

Everything is a mentor: If you are at zero in every way, whatever your personal zero may be, and have the passion for reinvention, everything you look at will be a metaphor for what you want to do. The tree you see, with roots you don't see and underground water that feeds it: it's all a metaphor for computer programming if you connect the dots.

And wherever you look, you will connect the dots.

e) *Don't worry if you don't have a passion for anything.*

Do what you do with love, whatever that might be for today, and success will naturally follow.

f) *Get your idea muscle in shape.*

Take baby steps. At first write just ten ideas a day. They can be bad. For example, ten things I like: ice cream, strawberries, cake, sleep, light, silence . . . you get the point. Do not worry. Write the ideas. Do it every day. The muscle will grow. Then write 20, then 100.

Some people tell us, "I can't. I just can't. I just have four or five ideas and then nothing else."

Our response is "Okay, you don't need to come up with ten ideas. You *need* to come up with twenty ideas!" You need to learn how to come up with *bad* ideas. The idea muscle grows stronger with repetition.

Then the ideas start to get better. Then the ideas flow. Then the idea muscle will turn into a machine. Then you will see the world for what it is: an ocean of creativity where everyone is clinging to the bottom, afraid to let go and float.

But you, my friend—your eyes are wide open.

You let go. And the ocean takes you home.

g) *Time it takes to reinvent yourself: five years.*

Here's a description of the five years:

Year One: You're flailing and reading everything and just starting to *do*.

Year Two: You know who you need to talk to and network with. You're *doing* every day. You finally know what the Monopoly board looks like in your new endeavors.

Year Three: You're good enough to start making money. It might not be a living yet.

Year Four: You're making a good living, and you can quit your day job.

Year Five: You're making wealth.

Sometimes you get frustrated in years one through four. You say, "Why isn't it happening yet?" That's okay. Just keep going. Or stop and pick a new field.

h) *Patience is the key.*

If your reinvention is faster or slower than five years, you are doing something wrong.

i) *It's not about the money, but money is a decent measuring stick.*

When people say, "It's not about the money," they should make sure they have a different measuring stick.

"What about just doing what you love?" There will be many days when you don't love what you are doing.

If you are doing it just for love, it will take much longer than five years. Often, we fall in love with what we are succeeding at. It's unclear if love comes first. Sometimes it's a back-and-forth, like any new relationship.

Happiness is just a positive perception by your brain. Some days you will be unhappy. Your brain is a tool you use. It's not who you are.

j) *When can I say to the world: "I do X!" where X is my new career?*
Today.

k) *When can I start doing X?*
Today.

If you want to paint, then sit in front of the canvas today and paint. Start buying 500 books, or getting them from the public library, one at a time, and reading them. Learn a little every day, and keep painting.

If you want to write do these three things: Read. Write. Take your favorite story by your favorite author and type it word for word. Ask yourself why he wrote each word. He's your mentor today.

If you want to start a business, write all the specs and details of the idea for your business. Reinvention starts today. Every day.

l) *How do I make money?*

By Year Three you've put in 5,000 to 7,000 hours of work. That's good enough to be in the top 200 to 300 people in the world in anything. The top 200 in almost any field make a living.

By Year Three you will know how to make money. By Year Four you will scale that up and make a living. Some people stop at Year Four.

By Year Five you're in the top 30 to 50 so you can make wealth.

m) *What is "it"? How do I know what I should do?*

Whatever area you feel like reading 500 books about. Go to the bookstore or the library and find it. If you get bored three months later, go back to the library.

It's okay to get disillusioned. That's what failure is about. Success is better than failure, but the biggest lessons are found in failure.

Very important: There's no rush. You will reinvent yourself many times in an interesting life. You will fail to reinvent many times also.

n) *Many reinventions make your life a book of stories instead of a textbook.*

Some people want the story of their life to be a textbook. For better or worse, most of us are books of stories.

The choices you make today will be in your biography tomorrow. Make interesting choices and you will have an interesting biography.

o) *The choices you make today will be in your biology tomorrow.*

Beware of anger—it causes dis-ease. If you encounter anger along the way, it means something got stuck within you. Sit in silence with the feeling; let it pass through you so you can remain open and ready to continue your reinvention journey.

p) *What if I like something obscure? Like biblical archaeology or 11th-century warfare?*

Repeat all of the steps above and in Year Five you will make wealth. We have no idea how. Don't look to find the end of the road when you are still at the very first step. Just walk the first one. Release the need to know how it will all happen.

q) *What if my family wants me to be an accountant?*

How many years of your life did you promise your family? Ten years? Your whole life? Then wait until the next life. The good thing is: you get to choose.

Choose freedom over family. Freedom over preconceptions. Freedom over government. Freedom over people pleasing. Then you will be pleased.

r) *My mentor wants me to do it his way.*

That's fine. Learn his way. Then do it *your* way. With respect.

Hopefully nobody has a gun to your head. If they do, you have to do it their way until the gun is put down.

s) *My spouse is worried about who will support/take care of the kids.*

You will. After you work 16 hours a day, seven days a week in a job you don't like, use your spare time to reinvent.

Someone who is reinventing *always* has spare time. Part of reinvention is collecting little bits and pieces of time and carving them the way you want them to be. That is the Power of No in action: you say no to the superfluous distractions because you must find some time for you.

t) *What if my friends think I'm crazy?*

What friends?

u) *What if I want to be an astronaut?*

That's not a reinvention; that's a specific job. If you like "outer space," there are many careers. Maybe Richard Branson wanted to be an astronaut. Then he started Virgin Galactic.

v) *What if I like to go out drinking and partying?*
Read this book again in a year.

w) *What if I'm busy cheating on my husband or wife or betraying a partner?*
Read this book again in two or three years when you are broke and jobless and nobody likes you.

x) *What if I have no skills at all?*
Read "B" again.

y) *What if I have no degree or I have a useless degree?*
Read "B" again.

z) *What if I have to focus on paying down my debt and mortgage?*
Read "S" again.

aa) *How come I always feel like I'm on the outside looking in?*
Albert Einstein was on the outside looking in. Nobody in the establishment would even hire him.
The highest form of creativity is born out of skepticism. Einstein didn't blindly follow the path of the time; he made his own.

bb) *I can't read 500 books. What one book should I read for inspiration?*
Give up.

cc) *What if I'm too sick to reinvent?*
Reinvention will boost every healthy chemical in your body: serotonin, dopamine, oxytocin. Keep moving forward and you might not get healthy but you will get healthier. Don't use health as an excuse.
Or reinvent your health first. Sleep more hours. Eat better. Exercise. These are key steps in reinvention.

dd) *What if my last partner screwed me and I'm still suing him?*
Stop litigating and never think about him again. Half the problem was you, not him.

ee) *What if I'm going to jail?*
Perfect. Reread "B." Read a lot of books in jail.

ff) *What if I'm shy?*
Make your weaknesses your strengths. Introverts listen better, focus better, and have ways of being more endearing.

gg) *What if I can't wait five years?*
If you plan on being alive in five years, you might as well start today.

hh) *How should I network?*
Make concentric circles. You're at the middle.
The next circle is friends and family.
The next circle is online communities.
The circle after that is meet-ups and coffees.
The circle after that is conferences and thought leaders.
The circle after that is mentors.
The circle after that is customers and wealth creators.
Start making your way through the circles.

ii) *What happens when I have ego about what I do?*
In 6 to 12 months you'll be back at "B."

jj) *What if I'm passionate about two things and I can't decide?*
Combine them and you'll be the best in the world at the combination.

kk) *What if I'm so excited I want to teach what I'm learning?*
Start teaching on YouTube. Start with an audience of one and see if it builds up.

ll) *What if I want to make money while I sleep?*
In Year Four, start outsourcing what you do.

mm) *How do I meet mentors and thought leaders?*
Once you have enough knowledge (after 100 to 200 books), write down ten ideas for 20 different potential mentors.

None of them will respond. Write down ten more ideas for 20 new mentors. Repeat every week.

Put together a newsletter for everyone who doesn't respond. Keep repeating until someone responds. Blog about your learning efforts. Build community around you being an expert.

nn) *What if I can't come up with ideas?*
Then keep practicing coming up with ideas. The idea muscle atrophies. You have to build it up.

It's hard for James to touch his toes if he hasn't been doing it every day. He has to try every day for a while before he can easily touch his toes (good thing Claudia is his yoga teacher). Don't expect to come up with good ideas on day one.

oo) *What else should I read?*
After books, you can read websites, forums, magazines. But most of that is garbage. Start with 500 books.

pp) *What if I do everything you say but it still doesn't seem like it's working?*

It will work. Just wait. Keep reinventing every day.

Don't try to find the end of the road. You can't see it in the fog. But you can see the next step and you *do* know that if you take that next step eventually you will get to the end of the road.

qq) *What if I get depressed?*

Sit in silence for one hour a day. You need to get back to your core.

If you think this sounds stupid, don't do it. Stay depressed.

rr) *What if I don't have time to sit in silence for one hour a day?*

Then sit in silence for two hours a day. This is not meditation. This is just sitting.

ss) *What if I get scared?*

If you're feeling overwhelmed, break it down. Sleep for eight to nine hours a night and never gossip. Sleep is the number-one key to successful health. It's not the only key; it's just number one. Some people write to me and say, "I only need four hours of sleep" or "In my country sleeping means laziness." Well, those people will fail and die young.

What about gossip? The brain biologically wants to have 150 friends. Then when you are with one of your friends, you can gossip about any of the other 149. If you don't have 150 friends, the brain wants to read gossip magazines until it thinks it has 150 friends.

Don't be as stupid as your brain.

tt) *What if I keep feeling like nothing ever works out for me?*
Spend ten minutes a day practicing gratitude. Don't suppress the fear. Notice the anger.

But also allow yourself to be grateful for the things you have. Anger is never inspiring but gratitude is. Gratitude is the bridge between your world and the parallel universe where all creative ideas live.

uu) *What if I have to deal with personal BS all the time?*
Find new people to be around.

Someone who is reinventing herself will constantly find people to try to bring her down. The brain is scared of reinvention because it might not be safe.

Biologically, the brain wants you to be safe, and reinvention is a risk. So it will throw people in your path who will try to stop you.

Learn how to say no.

vv) *What if I'm happy at my cubicle job?*
Good luck.

ww) *Why should I trust you—you've failed so many times?*
Don't trust us.

xx) *Will you be my mentors?*
You are reading this book. We are all reinventing our lives together.

We are all learning to say yes.

TIME TO SAY NO
TO THIS BOOK

JAMES: Last fall we were driving past the forests that lace themselves around the area where we live.

Death was everywhere.

We could see it on the trees. They were part green, part red, part orange, part yellow. Within a day or two the yellow leaves would be brown, and then they would die and fall off.

Claudia said, "It's beautiful. It's like the trees are on fire with leaves."

And it's true. Death is beautiful in the fall. And there are all sorts of metaphors throughout the history of poetry and romance about the meaning of summer turning into fall. The metaphors are sometimes sad, sometimes poignant, sometimes beautiful and peaceful, and sometimes dark . . . winter is around the corner. Cold and brittle and hateful.

We worship death.

When someone is about to die, we often want to know what their last words will be. We want to know for several reasons.

Mostly, it seems we want to know if they see anything special. If they can see through the veil between life and afterlife and tell us what is there. Maybe they think they see their mother or father or long-dead friends. Maybe the afterlife is one big happy reunion that lasts forever.

Who knows? We don't.

But, maybe even more important, we want to hear their last words to see if some wisdom has been revealed to them.

Let's back up for a second.

Remember when you were a kid? Doesn't matter how old. Ten years old. Fifteen years old. You pick.

Remember the last day of school for that year? It was awesome. There was no better day.

First off, there was this massive feeling of "Who cares?" because there was nothing left to care about. No exams, no assignments, no boring classes.

If I saw other kids I hated, then "Who cares?" I wouldn't be seeing them again for another three months. Heck, maybe I would never see them again. Three months was a long way away. There was no way to predict. Maybe they would move (or die—I didn't really care).

If I saw teachers, then big deal. There were no more tests. No more homework. It was the last day of school. There was no more time to do work. I never once saw a teacher and felt bad that I would never have her as a teacher again. My time with him or her was over.

And within hours I'd be riding my bike up the road. On the way to meet friends, or eat pizza, or go to a movie, or go swimming.

I didn't care about anything. The three months in front of me were like a wide trail that stretched into the forest farther than I could see. I could not make out the end.

I had nothing left to care about. What a relief. No worries about who I would run into, who would pick on me, who would gossip about me, what homework I still had to finish late at night on a Sunday when I'd rather be reading comic books. No facts I had to keep in my brain just long enough for a test and then watch those same facts spill onto the floor, never to be picked up ever again.

And I loved it. Nothing was better than that feeling. Rarely as an adult do I experience that feeling of such extreme relief. The finish line.

I used to get it when I was moving from one city to the next—the idea of the death of one part of my existence and the birth of a new one. But as I settled into marriage, kids, and a career, it was hard to find finality in that anymore. There was never any relief. For one thing, I am responsible for my family. And that lasts forever.

And I'm responsible for my career. Nobody else is. That won't end until my career does. Sometimes jobs change and you get a feeling of relief and newness and the end of what was stale and desperate about the old job, but that feeling goes quickly and transforms into nervousness about what comes next.

I want that relief I felt as a kid again.

But back to death.

It's like the last day of school all over again.

So we crowd around the bed of the person who is about to die and ask for those last words.

Recently a book about the last words of wisdom from some 100 dying people, and what their words had in common, has become popular. Another book that is very popular is *The Last Lecture* by Randy Pausch, a professor at Carnegie Mellon University who had terminal cancer and was giving the last lecture of his career—of his life.

Another book is *Tuesdays with Morrie*, about a man who spends time with another man who is close to death.

When you are close to death you get a perspective on what is important because you now have some relief from all of the things that are no longer important: like making sure you can feed yourself for years to come, or dealing with small political squabbles at work, or voting Democratic or Republican, or whatever it is you spend years and years of your waking life worried and anxious about.

There is a beauty to death, like the beauty of the leaves on the trees as summer turns to fall.

The leaves are like fire.

The words of the dying can light our minds on fire.

But we don't have to visit hospitals to get this wisdom. We can get it right now, wherever we are.

There's a saying: "Live life like it's your last day." Although I don't like that saying, let's try a little game.

— EXERCISE —
REBIRTH

- Lie down.

- Close your eyes and relax your body.

- Take a few deep, cleansing breaths, without forcing.

- Imagine that it is the time of your death. This is it. You've already said all of your good-byes.

- What will you be tomorrow? You might be nothing. You won't be your body. You won't be your thoughts since those are concocted with the help of the physical organ called your brain.

- We don't know what you will be. All you can do is list the things you won't be.

- List the things you won't worry about anymore. List the things you won't regret anymore.

- Love yourself for the gift you've given yourself: a life where you've learned many things. A life where you've been good and bad. A life where you've been lonely and depressed but also happy and fulfilled. It's been a roller coaster, hasn't it?! Love what you've been given.

- Picture an image of yourself and hug it. Kiss it good-bye. You've done a good job, and now it is time to go.

- Now feel that relief. Like it's the last day of school—only better.

At this point there is silence. Now you are the person with the words of wisdom. It's your turn to know what's important and what's not.

This infinite wisdom is in your mind right now.

Maybe tell yourself one or two sentences from this well of deep and infinite richness.

Write those words down. Keep them with you to remember the wisdom you have within.

This exercise is not morbid; tomorrow you will wake up and live life. You will go back to work and see the people you have political squabbles with, and every now and then the regrets will creep up and the anxieties will tickle the bottom of your heart.

So when you need to, close your eyes and come back to this moment. Come back to the moment when you hug yourself for a job well done on the life you've lived.

When you do this and you practice isolating the relief of being at the finish line, you will always be able to tap into that same resource of wisdom that so many famous books and "dying quotes" tap into.

For all of human history we have relied on that wisdom to know what's really important in life. To know who we really love. To know what we should really focus on in terms of our calling or our purpose.

Practice the feeling when you can. Maybe even every night before you go to sleep.

The more you tap into that feeling and that wisdom, the more you allow room for miracles to occur in your life. Miracles that normally get crowded out by the anxieties and regrets and worries and politics and fears of everyday life.

In those moments, you are the fire, you are the leaves on fire, you are the relief—*you* are the wisdom of the universe.

COMING TO YES

No, no, no, *no!*

One would think we're like mean parents, always saying no! to everything. Bad news. Bad people. Bad this, bad that.

But that's not what this is about.

This book is about *you*.

About the good things that can happen to you when you learn to say no. When you protect yourself from the people and situations that will hurt you. When you shield yourself from the stories and myths your colleagues, friends, family, and institutions use to control you. When you finally say no to the inner conditioning and psychology that your brain forces on you in its misguided attempts to protect you.

And when you work on the things that you can do: observe the role you play, notice your emotions, pay attention to your own spiritual growth.

There is a new world around you now. A world filled with love and innovation and abundance and creativity.

This is the world you say yes to.

I (Claudia) am not perfect. Not by any stretch of the imagination. But I will tell you one thing I have learned over the years, whenever I find myself in that place where I can't believe I did something "so bad," and not only that, but also that I did it "again." That is a bummer, isn't it? When we do something that hurts us and we realize it is not the first time. *How could I?*

The one thing I have noticed is that every time I hurt myself, there was a No I did not respect.

I (James) have often said yes before I was ready. I would say yes to relationships that I wasn't mature enough to handle. Or yes to opportunities that I squandered.

Or yes to doing things I did not want to do.

What happens during those moments? You can get sick. You can squander the energy you build up. You can physically hurt yourself. You can get depressed. You can fail.

You end up spending precious time when you could've been making time precious.

The Power of No is about building *your* power from the core outward. It's about harnessing the energy in the universe so you become a living spiritual battery, filled with creativity and abundance and maturity and love.

Then when you say yes, it's like dropping a pebble in the center of the ocean. Ultimately the ripples from that Yes will ripple outward and hit every shore.

They will change the world.

They will change *you.*

ABOUT THE AUTHORS

JAMES ALTUCHER is a successful entrepreneur, chess master, spiritual teacher, and writer. He has started and run more than 20 companies, some of which failed, several of which he sold for large exits.

But more important, James has been inspiring people through hundreds of events, through his books, and through weekly Q&A Twitter sessions, speaking on topics including stress, fear, anxiety, business, love, money, and relationships.

His writing has appeared in many major national media outlets, including *The Wall Street Journal,* ABC, the *New York Observer, Elephant Journal, Tech Crunch,* and *Thought Catalog.*

His blog, The Altucher Confidential, has attracted more than 15 million readers since its launch in 2010. He is the author of 12 books, including the bestseller *Choose Yourself* and *I Was Blind but Now I See.* Join him at JamesAltucher.com or on Twitter @Jaltucher.

CLAUDIA AZULA ALTUCHER is an author and teacher of yoga, meditation, and ancient spiritual principles.

She is the author of *21 Things to Know Before Starting an Ashtanga Yoga Practice.* She also writes for many media outlets, including *Thought Catalog, Mantra Yoga + Health* magazine, *Elephant Journal,* and *MyLifeYoga.*

Claudia also runs yoga and spiritual retreats around the country. Join her at ClaudiaYoga.com or on Twitter @ClaudiaYoga.

HAY HOUSE TITLES
OF RELATED INTEREST

YOU CAN HEAL YOUR LIFE, the movie,
starring Louise Hay & Friends
(available as a 1-DVD program, an expanded 2-DVD set, and an
online streaming video)
Learn more at: www.hayhouse.com/louise-movie

THE SHIFT, the movie, starring Dr. Wayne W. Dyer
(available as a 1-DVD program, an expanded 2-DVD set, and an
online streaming video)
Learn more at: www.hayhouse.com/the-shift-movie

*HOW TO STAY SANE IN A CRAZY WORLD: A Modern Book of
Hours to Soothe the Soul,* by Sophia Stuart

*MIND CALM: The Modern-Day Meditation Technique That Proves the
Secret to Success Is Stillness,* by Sandy C. Newbigging

*MIRACLES NOW: 108 Life-Changing Tools for Less Stress, More Flow,
and Finding Your True Purpose,* by Gabrielle Bernstein

*NOTHING CHANGES UNTIL YOU DO: A Guide to Self-Compassion
and Getting Out of Your Own Way,* by Mike Robbins

All of the above are available at your local bookstore,
or may be ordered by contacting Hay House (see next page).